Elder Law
Estate Planning

Michael Ettinger
Attorney and Counselor at Law

Copyright © 2015 by Michael Ettinger

Disclaimer: This publication contains the opinions and ideas of its author. It is intended to provide helpful and informative materials on the subject matter covered. It is sold with the understanding that the author and publisher are not engaged in rendering professional services in the book. If the reader requires personal assistance or advice, a competent professional should be consulted.

Elder Law Estate Planning is available at special quantity discounts for bulk purchases for sales promotions, premiums, fund-raising, or educational use. Special books, or book excerpts, can also be created to fit specific needs.

For details, write: Ettinger Law Firm, 125 Wolf Road, Albany, New York 12205.

Acknowledgements

This writer would like to thank the following persons for their assistance in bringing this book to fruition. Bonnie Kraham, Attorney at Law, and Lisa M. Govel, Medicaid Supervisor, Ettinger Law Firm, for their editorial support; and Patricia Brown, Firm Manager, Ettinger Law Firm, for many helpful suggestions as well as for managing logistics. Special thanks as well to the dedicated attorneys, paralegals and administrative professionals at Ettinger Law Firm who help put the essential information contained in this book into practice through their dealings with the public every day.

March, 2015

For Ian, Zoë and Cameron

Contents

Medicaid Planning Strategies

Estate Administration Upon Death

Introduction

Introduction

Why Planning for Disability is More Important than Planning for Death

Wills have been around for a long time, almost five hundred years now. They were invented by King Henry VIII of England. He required a court proceeding on death called "probate" which literally means to prove the validity of the will. In other words, proof is required in court that the creator of the will was of sound mind, memory and understanding, was not under any fraud or undue influence, was able to read, write and converse in the English language, etc. Although the rationale for going to court has long since passed, in law the wheels of change grind every so slowly. Too many people still think that a will is all the "estate planning" they need. Yet wills often fail to take into account the majority of a client's assets. Wills do not govern assets passing by beneficiary designation, such as IRA's, life insurance and annuities. Furthermore, clients are increasingly using POD (pay on death), TOD (transfer on death) and ITF (in trust for) designations to entirely bypass the will and the antiquated probate system. As a result, in many cases the bulk of a client's estate is actually "unplanned", except to avoid probate. By this we mean that the assets may still be unprotected from a Medicaid "spend down" if the client one day needs nursing home care; the assets are not protected from the heirs' divorces, lawsuits and creditors; the assets are not structured to stay in the bloodline to the client's grandchildren and the assets are not protected from a spouse's later remarriage.

Perhaps the biggest drawback to relying on a will as an "estate plan" is that it utterly fails to address the senior client's most important issue – planning for disability. The will only takes effect on death. As such, it is not a plan for disability. Of course many people who have wills become disabled, so what happens in these cases? If you do not have an adequate plan for disability the state has written a plan for you. You've probably heard of it. It's called guardianship. If you are unable to handle your affairs for any reason, a judge of the county in which you reside may step in and appoint someone to handle your legal and financial affairs for you, called a legal guardian. Who is the judge going to choose? Of course that is going to be up to the judge, but it may not be who you would think. Your adult children? Some judges feel your children have a conflict – if they spend the money on you it is coming out of their inheritance. Judges often pick someone such as a local attorney who "knows the system". Your writer has been chosen for this purpose. The first thing a guardian does is collect up all the assets -- stocks, bonds, bank accounts, IRA's, etc. and often move them to an advisor or firm that the guardian is comfortable with. After all, the guardian must file an annual accounting of the assets under management and may be held liable for any losses. The greater problem with guardianship, however, is that people are increasingly recovering from disabilities such as strokes, heart attacks and serious operations. Now, when you recover, do you think you can just take back your assets whenever you feel ready? Of course not. There is a standing court order giving the guardian control over those assets. To get back control of your assets, you have to go back to court, have a trial, and prove to the judge's satisfaction that you are able to handle your affairs. If you are successful, then the judge cancels the order and puts you back in charge.

Can you see yourself here? You're in your eighties or nineties in court fighting to get your own assets back? Worse, sometimes the legal guardian is opposing you. Just not a happy place to be and not a place where our clients find themselves because they almost all use trusts rather than wills.

As we shall see, the first reason to use a trust is that it avoids a guardianship proceeding -- virtually guaranteeing you will get the person or persons you want to handle your affairs if you become disabled -- usually one or more of your adult children.

Why is it so important to have your people in charge in the event of disability? First, a little background. In all of the thousands elder law estate plans we have created over the years, you the client choose someone you trust, or two people acting together, and authorize them to move assets out of your name if you should become disabled. It's call the "unlimited gifting power". Why do we need to give someone an unlimited gifting power? Because we know that if our client one day needs to go into a nursing facility, under Medicaid law it's "move it or lose it". Here, we're talking about transferring real estate, stocks, bonds, mutual funds, bank accounts and the like, often worth hundreds of thousands of dollars or more. As discussed in later chapters, there are numerous techniques and strategies available to protect assets, even on the nursing home doorstep, with the assistance of a qualified elder law estate planning attorney.

Of course you can expect your children to act in your family's best interests. Can you count on a legal guardian to do so? Not always. A legal guardian is required to consider the interests of the person they are guardian for. Often that means they simply spend the assets on you until there is nothing left. While they can, in theory, apply to the court to protect assets, in your writer's experience they often fail to do so (having no stake in the matter, as your family would). In other cases, they do apply for permission to transfer and protect assets and the judge turns them down, a situation your writer has observed first hand.

Some people believe a power of attorney avoids guardianship. It is certainly an important document to have. It allows someone to handle your legal and financial affairs if you become incapacitated. Nevertheless, a power of attorney does not defeat a guardianship proceeding. Judges have the power to cancel your power of attorney and appoint someone else. Fortunately, a judge has no power to cancel or revoke a trust. While a guardianship trumps a power of attorney, a trust trumps a guardianship.

Planning for disability is primary since it is for you. Planning for death is for who? Them, whoever they may be. You come first. With nursing homes costing up to fifteen thousand dollars a month these days, and the average nursing home stay lasting forty-two months, six hundred and thirty thousand dollars or more may be required. Further, you are responsible for up to five years (or beyond that if you fail to take steps to protect assets) which is nine hundred thousand dollars. If you don't have a plan for disability to protect your assets, who gets it after you're gone may be moot. So far as a will being an estate plan then, it's like the old saying, "The operation was a success, but the patient died." In other words, we had a great estate plan but there was no estate left.

In this author's experience, almost everyone wants the same three things in the event of disability. First, they want their family or others they trust in charge, not the state. Second, they want to be able to take back control of their assets whenever they feel ready. They do not want to be going to court asking a judge for permission to get their own assets, which permission may be denied. Finally, they do not want to see the nest egg they built up over thirty, forty, fifty or more years disappear in three or four years because nursing homes are now costing up to fifteen thousand dollars a month.

For the foregoing reasons, we are of the opinion that wills have become obsolete, at least for people sixty plus. We term this new field of law "Elder Law Estate Planning". Elder law is disability planning to put the people you choose in charge and to protect some or all of your assets from long-term care costs. Estate planning is death planning to make sure your assets go to whom you want, when you want and the way you want with the least amount of taxes and legal fees possible. We know that estate planning is essential since the mortality rate is one hundred percent, but we also know that about half of our clients will become disabled. We just don't know which half so we must make sure that everyone has an elder law asset protection plan for their later years as well.

In the following chapters you will learn what it means to have an "elder law estate plan" and why it is an essential plan for the middle class senior to have.

Elder Law Estate Planning

1

What is Elder Law Estate Planning?

What is Elder Law Estate Planning?

"Elder Law Estate Planning" is a niche area of the law which combines the features of elder law and estate planning that pertain most to the needs of the middle class.

Estate planning was originally for the wealthy few. Middle class families did not consider themselves as having "estates" to plan. During the Reagan years (1980-1988), a great economic expansion occurred, raising the asset level of the middle class into the realm of estate planning. With middle class people suddenly exposed to "estate taxes", the need arose for estate planning, to reduce or eliminate those taxes. A few years later, in 1991, the American Association of Retired Persons (AARP) published "A Consumer

Report on Probate" which concluded that probate was a process to be avoided, in all but the most exceptional cases. This marked the beginning of the end of traditional will planning and started the "living trust revolution". AARP recommended that families start using trusts rather than wills, to avoid probate and save their beneficiaries tens of thousands of dollars in the estate settlement process.

Since 1991, tens of millions of people have set up trusts to:

- Save time and money in settling the estate

- Avoid legal guardianship if they become disabled

- Avoid having their personal and financial matters made public

- Reduce the chance of a "will contest"

- Keep control in their family and out of the court system

At about the same time as living trust planning became popular, the field of elder law emerged to help people navigate the increased complexity of state Medicaid rules and regulations, the soaring costs of nursing home stays, and the fact that people were living considerably longer.

Historically, estate planning was handled primarily by "white shoe" law firms in the deep canyons of downtown Manhattan, while elder law planning emerged out of the Department of Social Services.

State employees began to take their expertise in Medicaid rules and regulations into the private sector.

To this day, these two fields continue to grow independently of each other, sometimes to the detriment of the clients lawyers are meant to serve. Estate planning lawyers mostly see estates averaging from the low hundreds of thousands to about one million dollars. Families with estates under one million dollars often cannot afford long-term care insurance. They may now or later need a Medicaid Asset Protection Trust (MAPT) (Chapter 20) to protect their estates from being depleted in the event a nursing home is required. Since the estate planning attorney is often unfamiliar with elder law, the client never gets the MAPT they need, and the estate plan to avoid probate proves useless when a nursing home stay ends up consuming all of the assets.

For the couple with over one million dollars in assets, while they may more often be able to afford long-term care insurance, sometimes either one or both of them are uninsurable due to health reasons or they have waited until age seventy or so and the premiums are too high. Perhaps what they really need is the MAPT, to protect the assets from nursing home costs, but they never get one because the estate planning lawyer is not experienced or trained in drafting these documents.

What happens when the estate planning client actually becomes disabled and needs long-term care? They, or the family, often consult with the estate planning lawyer who prepared their plan, but who may be unable to help them, due to his or her unfamiliarity with state Medicaid rules. Many families lose assets that might have been saved. Unknown to the estate planning attorney, elder law attorneys have developed numerous techniques to protect hard won assets, even when the nursing home is imminent, such as "spousal refusal" and the "gift and loan" strategy, discussed in the chapters that follow.

On the other side of the coin, what happens when the older single or couple meets with an elder law attorney instead of an estate planning attorney? These clients are usually sixty-five or over, and are looking for asset protection. The elder law attorney knows how to create a MAPT and often recommends them. However, on the estate planning side of matters, the elder law attorney may miss the need to set up two trusts for the couple to avoid the estate tax, if they are exposed to that liability. He or she may have little knowledge about estate planning for second marriages, a growing segment of the population, or using Inheritance Trusts to keep the assets in the blood and protect the inheritance from children's divorces, lawsuits, and creditors.

While some of the family's needs may be met, such as asset protection, other needs are left unserved, often because the clients are unaware that these two fields of law complement and overlap one another. In other words, they may get what they want but not necessarily what they need. These oversights are often visited on the heirs.

Your writer made the conscious decision over twenty years ago to develop expertise in these two fields of law simultaneously. This has proven to be invaluable to thousands of families. Clients who originally came in for estate planning services later became elder law clients, converting their revocable living trust estate plans into MAPT's as they got older or, through the use of Medicaid planning services, ended up protecting their assets when the need for nursing home care actually arose.

Looking back on our experiences in over ten thousand cases at Ettinger Law Firm, we conclude that we have assisted in the creation of a new niche legal field, "Elder Law Estate Planning".

We define this area of law as:

- Getting your assets to your heirs, when you want and the way you want, with the least amount of taxes and legal fees possible

- Keeping those assets in the blood for your grandchildren and, in the meantime, protecting those assets from your children's divorces, lawsuits, and creditors

- Protecting your assets from the costs of long-term care and qualifying you for government benefits available to pay for that care

While estate planning involves tools for well-to-do families, with acronyms like GRITS, GRATS, and GRUTS, and where elder law serves the diverse needs of our growing senior population, including the less fortunate, through Medicaid, Medicare and Social Security, "Elder Law Estate Planning" addresses the concerns of the vast majority in the middle. It is those people who are the subject of this book.

2

Pitfalls of Will Planning

So many clients are advised that they need a will. In fact, will planning is becoming obsolete for persons over sixty for many reasons.

Instead of actually solving problems, wills often create them. First, they must be proven to be valid in a court proceeding, the infamous probate. Court proceedings may be expensive, time-consuming and things often go wrong. Also, when the client dies, that will is usually out-of-date, having been created decades before. The executors may be the wrong persons, the beneficiaries or their percentages may be wrong or other changes in the family have not been taken into account.

Notice of the court proceeding must be given to certain relatives who may be difficult or impossible to locate. Complications arise with relatives in foreign countries who may need to go to the American Consulate for notarization or "consularization" of legal documents. If there is a disabled child, the court will appoint a lawyer to represent that heir's interests, including preparing a report to the court, and your estate must pay that attorney's fees.

Proof problems with the will may lead to delays preventing needed funds from getting to surviving spouses or children. It is fairly common for real estate to be tied up, while the probate process drags on, causing potential buyers to be lost. In some cases, stock cannot be sold even though it may be falling in value rapidly. Law firms routinely find they must commence probate proceedings as a courtesy for families who cannot afford the legal fees to get the matter started. The cost of court proceedings today may be expected to be in the five figure range.

Two other pitfalls of will planning bear mentioning. First, since the will is filed in court, it becomes a public record. Anyone may go to the courthouse and order a copy of your will to see what you had and who you left it to. Secondly, since notice must be given to the heirs you may have left out, or left less than they may feel they are entitled to, you run the risk of a will contest if your estate is distributed in anything but equal shares.

When you are in probate court, who is in charge? The judge, not you or your lawyer. Don't suppose that the judge will always act in your best interests, as the court may have other interests to consider.

Always better to stay out of court if you can. By using a living trust, instead of a will, you avoid probate court proceedings and keep control, or at least control rests with those you have chosen, if you die or become disabled. The expenses are sufficiently less without court proceedings that you may save tens of thousands of dollars.

The other problem with a will? It only takes effect when you die. Today, about half of all people eventually become disabled. Since the will does not provide for disability, you risk guardianship proceedings. These proceedings occur later in life when someone becomes unable to handle their affairs and does not have an adequate plan set up for disability. In a guardianship, the court will appoint someone to handle your affairs. Not only may it not be the person you would have chosen, it may not even be someone you know. Trusts, which take effect while you are living, are considered a highly effective tool to avoid guardianship proceedings so that the person or persons you choose will be in charge. This way, you may be certain that your best interests will be looked after.

In short, when someone tells you that you need a will, think again. It may be a trust that you need instead.

"During my life, and now by my will and codicils, I have given considerable sums of money to promote public and humanitarian causes which have had my deliberate and sympathetic interest. If any of my children think excessive such gifts of mine outside of the family, I ask them to remember not only the merit of the causes and the corresponding usefulness of the gifts but also the dominating ideals of my life.

They should never forget the dangers which unfortunately attend the inheritance of large fortunes, even though the money come from the painstaking affections of a father. I beg of them to remember that such danger lies not only in the obvious temptation to enervating luxury, but in the inducement...to withdraw from the wholesome duty of vigorous, serious, useful work. In my opinion a life not largely dedicated to such work cannot be happy and honorable. And to such it is my earnest hope — and will be to my death — that my children shall, so far as their strength permits, be steadfastly devoted."

Joseph Pulitzer, Will, in James Wyman Barret,
Joseph Pulitzer and His World 295-96 (1941)

3

The Five Steps to an Elder Law Estate Plan

Overview

Practicing elder law estate planning is one of the most enjoyable and professionally rewarding careers an attorney may choose. Imagine a practice area where your clients respect your knowledge and treat you with kindness and courtesy. They pay your fees in a timely fashion and tell their friends how much they have enjoyed working with you and your firm. At the same time, you are rarely facing the pressure of a deadline, much less an adversarial attorney on the other side of a matter trying to best you. In most instances, you are acting in the capacity of a counselor at law (trusted advisor) rather than an attorney at law (professional representative).

We spend our days meeting with clients, discussing their lives and their families and addressing their fears and concerns. Through our knowledge, training, experience and imagination, we craft solutions, occasionally elegant ones, to the age old problem of passing assets from one generation to another as quickly and painlessly as possible.

At the same time, we also seek to protect those assets from being depleted by taxes, legal fees and nursing home costs to the extent the law allows.

The end result of this process is a client who feels safe and secure in the knowledge that, in the event of death or disability, they have all their bases covered. Having achieved peace of mind that their future is well planned and in good hands, they can get on with the business of enjoying their lives. For the attorney, a happy and satisfied client has been added to the practice and another potentially lifelong and mutually rewarding relationship has begun. Let's look at the strategies and techniques we use to achieve this enviable state of affairs.

Major Issues Facing Senior Clients Today

One of the ways that we help clients is in setting up a comprehensive plan so they may avoid court proceedings upon death or in the event of disability. Trusts are used in place of wills for older persons since they do not require court proceedings to settle the estate. Trusts also avoid the foreign probate proceeding required for property owned in another state, known as ancillary probate. This saves the family time in settling the estate as well as the high costs of legal proceedings. In addition, since revocable living trusts, unlike wills, take effect during the grantor's lifetime, the client may stipulate which persons take over in the event of their disability. Planning ahead helps maintain control in the family or with trusted advisors and avoids a situation that may not be in the client's best interest. For example, in the event of a disability where no plan has been put in place, an application to the court may be required in order to have a legal guardian appointed for the disabled person. This may not be the person the client would have chosen. In such a case, assets may not be transferred to protect them from being spent down for nursing home costs without court permission, which may or may not be granted.

Another area in which we assist the client is in saving state estate taxes, for married couples by using the two-trust technique. Assets are divided as evenly as practicable between each of the spouse's trusts. While the surviving spouse has the use and enjoyment of the deceased spouse's trust, the assets of that trust bypass the estate of the surviving spouse and go directly to the named beneficiaries when the second spouse dies. The two trusts are known as "disclaimer trusts", discussed in Chapter 13. Tens to hundreds of thousands of dollars, or more, in potential estate taxes may be saved, depending on the size of the estate. Furthermore, the revocable living trust avoids the two probates that would occur were the clients to use wills, as the couple's estate must be settled after the death of each spouse in order to save estate taxes.

We also help to protect assets from being depleted due to nursing home costs. Medicaid Asset Protection Trusts (MAPT's) may be established, subject to a five-year look-back period, to protect the client's home and other assets from having to be spent down due to the high cost of nursing home care. Elder law attorneys use Medicaid asset and transfer rules to protect assets in the event a client requires nursing home care but has done no pre-planning. Through the use of Medicaid annuities, the "gift and loan" strategy and Caregiver Agreements, significant assets may be protected despite the five-year look-back, even when the client may be on the nursing home doorstep. These techniques are discussed in later chapters.

The Five Steps to an Elder Law Estate Plan

Step One: Understanding the Family Dynamics

The first step in an elder law estate planning matter is to gain an understanding of the client's family dynamics. If there are children, which is usually the case, we need to determine whether or not they are married. Is it a first or second marriage? Do they have any children from a previous marriage or do their spouses? What kind of work do they do, and where do they live? Do they get along with each other and with the parent clients? We are looking to determine which family members do not get along with which others and what the reasons may be. This goes a long way toward helping us decide who should make medical decisions and who should handle legal and financial affairs. Should it be one of them or more than one? How should the estate be divided? Is the client himself in a second marriage? Which children, if any, are his, hers, or theirs? Sometimes all three instances may occur in the same couple. Here, further exploration of the family functioning will be needed as the potential for hurt feelings, conflicts of interest, and misunderstandings multiplies. In addition, great care must be taken to develop a plan for management, control, and distribution of the estate that will not only be fair to the children from a previous marriage but will be seen to be fair as well. At times, the assistance of the professional advisor in acting as trustee may be invaluable in helping to keep the peace between family members. Finally, this step will also flesh out whether there are any dependents with special needs and which family members and assets might be best suited to provide for such children.

Step Two: Reviewing Existing Estate Planning Documents

The second step in an elder law estate planning matter is to review any prior estate planning documents the client may have, such as a will, trust, power of attorney, health care proxy and living will, to determine whether they are legally sufficient and reflect the client's current wishes or whether they are outdated. Some basic elder law estate planning questions are also addressed at this time such as:

a. Is the client a US citizen? This may impinge on the client's ability to save estate taxes.

b. Is the client expecting to receive an inheritance? This knowledge helps in preparing a plan that will address not only the assets that the client has now but what they may have in the future.

c. Does the client have long-term care insurance? If so, the attorney will want to review the policy and determine whether it provides an adequate benefit considering the client's other assets and income, whether it takes inflation into account, and whether it is upgradable. This will allow the practitioner to decide whether other asset protection strategies may be needed now or later.

d. Does the client need financial planning? Many clients that come into the attorney's office have never had professional financial advice or are dissatisfied with their current advisors. They may need help understanding the assets they have or with organizing and consolidating them for ease of administration. They may also be concerned with not having enough income to last for the rest of their lives. The elder law estate planning attorney will typically know a number of capable financial planners who are experienced with the needs and wishes of the senior client, including (1) secure investments with protection of principal, and (2) assets that tend to maximize income.

Step Three: Reviewing the Client's Assets

The third step is to obtain a complete list of the client's assets, including how they are titled, their value, whether they are qualified investments, such as IRA's and 401(k)'s and, if they have beneficiary designations, who those beneficiaries are. Armed with this information, the counsellor is in a position to determine whether the estate will be subject to estate taxes, both state and federal, and may begin to formulate a strategy to reduce or eliminate those taxes to the extent the law allows. This will often lead to shifting assets between spouses and their trusts, changing beneficiary designations, and, with discretion, sometimes trying to determine which spouse might pass away first so as to effect the greatest possible tax savings. Ideally, the attorney should have the client fill out a confidential financial questionnaire prior to the initial consultation.

Step Four: Developing the Elder Law Estate Plan

The fourth step is to determine, with input from the client, who should make medical decisions for the client if they are unable to, i.e. the health care proxy, and who should be appointed to handle legal and financial affairs, i.e. the power of attorney, in the event of the client's incapacity. Next, we will consider what type of trust, if any, should be used, or whether a simple will would suffice, who should be the trustees (for a trust) or executors (for a will), and what the plan of distribution should be. In order to avoid a conflict, the trustees who are chosen in lieu of the grantor should be the same persons named on the power of attorney. At this point, great care should also be taken to ensure that the feelings of the heirs will not be hurt. Good estate planning looks at the client's estate from the heirs' point of view as well as the client's. For example, if there are three children, it may be preferable that one be named as trustee or executor, as three are usually too cumbersome and if the client chooses only two, then they are leaving one out. If there are four or five children, we prefer to see two trustees or executors chosen. This way, the pressure will be reduced on just the one having to answer to all the others. More importantly, the others will feel more secure with two siblings jointly looking after their interests.

Not all estates need to be distributed equally. An old adage in estate planning goes like this "There's nothing so unequal as the equal treatment of unequals".

If the distribution is to be unequal, it may need to be discussed with the affected children ahead of time to forestall any ill will or even litigation after the parents have died. By considering the relative ages of the children, where they live, and their relationships amongst each other and with their parents, the advisor will generally find a way to craft a plan that accommodates the needs and desires of all parties concerned. Some of the techniques we find useful in this context are to offer a delayed distribution, such as twenty percent upon the death of the grantor, one-half of the remaining balance after five years, and the remainder after ten years. These same percentages may also be used at stated ages, such as thirty, thirty-five, and forty. Also, when leaving percentages of the estate, unless it is simply to the children in equal shares, it is often useful to determine the monetary value of those percentages in the client's current estate. This will allow the client to see whether the amount is truly what they wish to bequeath. Percentage bequests to charities should be avoided so that the family may avoid the possibility of having to account to the charity for the expenses of administering the estate.

In terms of the type of trust, we are generally looking at several options for most clients. For couples, it is important to determine whether there should be one trust or two. In order to avoid or reduce estate taxes, there should be two trusts for spouses whose estates exceed or may at a later date exceed the state and/or federal estate tax threshold. Should the trust be revocable or irrevocable? The latter is important for protecting assets from nursing home expenses subject to the five-year look-back period. Primary features of the irrevocable Medicaid Asset Protection Trust (MAPT) are that neither the grantor nor the grantor's spouse may be the trustee and that these trusts are "income-only" trusts. Most people choose one or more of their adult children to act as trustees of the MAPT. Since principal is not available to the grantor, the client will not want to put all of their assets into such a trust. Assets that should be left out are IRA's, 401(k)'s, 403(b)'s, etc. The principal of these qualified assets are generally exempt from Medicaid and should not be placed into a trust, as this would create a taxable event requiring income taxes to be paid on all of the qualified money. If the institutionalized client has a spouse in the community, up to about one hundred and twenty thousand dollars may also be exempted. Notwithstanding that the home, at least up to a little more than eight hundred thousand dollars in equity, is exempt if the community spouse is living there, it is generally a good idea to protect the home now rather than to wait until the first spouse has passed, due to the five-year look-back period. It should be noted that the look-back means that from the time assets are transferred to the MAPT, it takes five years before they are exempt, or protected from being required to be spent down on the ill person's care before they qualify for Medicaid benefits. What if the client does not make the five years? Imagine that the client must go into the nursing home four years after the trust has been established. In such a case, by privately paying the nursing facility for the one year remaining, the family will be eligible for Medicaid after just the remaining year of the five-year penalty period has expired.

Although the MAPT is termed irrevocable, the home may still be sold or other trust assets traded. This does not restart the five year look-back. The trust itself, through the actions of the trustees, may sell the house and purchase a condominium in the name of the trust so that the asset is still protected. The trust may sell one stock and buy another. For those clients who may wish to continue trading on their own, the adult child trustee may sign a third party authorization with the brokerage firm authorizing the parent to continue trading on the account. Sometimes this is simply done online with the parent using the PIN on the account. The trust continues to pay all income (i.e., interest and dividends) to the parent grantor. As such, the irrevocable trust payments should not affect the client's lifestyle when added to any pensions, social security, and IRA or other qualified distributions the client continues receiving from outside the trust. Homeowners insurance should be modified to add the trustees, who are now on the deed, as additional insureds. MAPT's are discussed in more detail in Chapters 20 and 22.

If there is a disabled child, consideration will be given to creating a Special Needs Trust (Chapter 7), which will pay over and above what the child may be receiving in government benefits, especially social security income and Medicaid, so that the inheritance will not disqualify them from those benefits.

With the size of estates having grown today to where middle class families are leaving substantial bequests to their children (depending, of course, on how many children they have), the trend is toward establishing trusts for the children to keep the inheritance in the bloodline. Variously termed Inheritance Trusts, Heritage Trusts, or Dynasty Trusts, these trusts may contain additional features, such as protecting the inheritance from a child's divorce, lawsuits and creditors during their lifetimes, and estate taxes when they die. The primary feature of all of these trusts for the heirs, however, is to provide that when the child dies, in most cases many years after the parent, the hard-earned assets of the family will not pass to an in-law who may get remarried and eventually share assets with a stranger, but rather to the grantor's grandchildren. On the other hand, if the client wishes to favor the son-in-law or daughter-in-law, they may choose to provide that the trust, or a portion of it, continue as an "income only" trust for their adult child's surviving spouse for their lifetime, and only thereafter to the grantor's grandchildren. Inheritance Trusts are discussed in Chapter 6.

Other key areas for discussion in developing the elder law estate plan are second marriage planning (Chapter 8), planning for singles and couples without children (Chapter 9), protecting assets for spendthrift children (Chapter 10), and planning for same sex couples (Chapter 11).

Step Five: Executing and Maintaining the Plan

At the meeting to execute the elder law estate plan, the documents are reviewed with the client, explanations are given and questions are answered. Many practitioners favor sending the documents ahead of time for their clients' review. While there are advantages to this practice, we have found the clients are often overwhelmed by the legal documents and prefer to limit the practice to those instances where it is specifically requested.

After execution, including signing new deeds transferring real property into the trust, the client is advised how to transfer title of their investments and bank accounts to the trust. Similarly, beneficiary designations on annuities, life insurance policies and sometimes on IRA's and other qualified plans are often changed to the client's trust or to the children's Inheritance Trusts. In the event there is more than one trust being executed, which assets are left to which trust, and why, are explained to the client as part of the funding process.

Finally, the elder law estate plan is reviewed every three years for changes in the law as well as changes in the lives of the clients and their families. Inherent in the plan is the ability of the "hybrid" elder law estate planning firm to address Medicaid asset protection issues, either by planning ahead due to advancing years or, in the event of an "immediate need", when a crisis arises and the family has failed to take action in advance. Medicaid planning strategies, key tools in the elder law estate planning attorney's toolbox, are discussed in Chapters 19 through 28.

At our firm, we believe not only reviewing the plan every three years, but also in building the attorney-client relationship. Additional touchpoints are sending the client a weekly email on some interesting or important topic, inviting the client to an event every other year to update them on the law, as well as inviting their net of kin to "meet the lawyer", and providing ongoing monitoring of their plan for law changes that may affect them. This way, the elder law estate plan is far more likely to address their situation when they may need to use it in the future. Indeed, through the monitoring and review process the elder law estate plan is designed to work when the client needs it, not when they wrote it, perhaps decades earlier.

4

The Two Biggest Mistakes in Elder Law Estate Planning

1. Failure to address all of the issues.

A comprehensive review of the client's situation should address planning for disability as well as for death, including minimizing or avoiding estate taxes and legal fees and proceedings. A plan should be in place to protect assets from nursing home costs. Like a chess player, counsel should look ahead two or three moves in order to determine what may happen in the future. For example, attorneys will too often place a majority of the assets in the wife's name or in her trust in light of the husband having significant IRA or any qualified assets in his account. However, since the husband is often older and has a shorter life expectancy, this may result in the IRA type assets rolling over to the wife, all of the couple's assets ending up in the wife's estate, and no estate tax savings effected. Another example would be where the client's children are in a second marriage but have children (the client's grandchildren) from a previous marriage. Unless planning is done with Inheritance Trusts (Chapter 7) for the client's children, a situation may occur one day where the client's child predeceases their second spouse, all assets pass to the second spouse, and the client's grandchildren, from a son or daughter's prior marriage, are denied any benefit from the grantor's estate.

2. Failure to Regularly Review the Elder Law Estate Plan

At a minimum, each client's estate plan should be reviewed every three years to determine whether changes in the client's personal life, such as their health, assets, or family history (births, deaths, marriages, divorces, etc.) impact the plan. It is unrealistic to expect a plan established today to be effective ten, twenty, thirty, or more years in the future. Over time, clients will want to change their back-up trustees or plan of distribution. They may wish to add Inheritance Trusts for their children. They might, after a number of years, wish to change from a revocable trust to a MAPT because they were unable or unwilling to obtain long-term care insurance. The client will benefit from having a plan better suited to their current needs at any given time.

Despite the knowledge and earnestness of some of the best practitioners in the land, clients sometimes do not act on the advice given. Experienced attorneys know not to take it personally when clients choose to ignore their advice or perhaps choose other counsel. People don't always do what they need to, they do what they want to do. A ninety-three year old client once told us that she "wanted to think about it" so far as planning her affairs. Experience tells us that this client is not ready to plan at the present time, despite her advanced years, and we must respect that choice. On the other hand, we recall a client coming in to see us eleven years after their initial consultation stating that they were now ready to proceed. We prepared their estate plan.

5

Components of an
Elder Law Estate Plan

For most clients, an Elder Law Estate Plan consists of the following documents and features:

1. A Revocable Living Trust (RLT) or an Irrevocable Medicaid Asset Protection Trust (MAPT)

Generally the client will have one of these trusts or the other, not both. The MAPT is used where protection of assets is required in the absence of long-term care insurance. For married couples with estates over the estate tax exemption, state and/or Federal, two trusts may be required, one for each spouse, to create two estates thereby doubling the exemption from estate taxes. Where clients wish to protect the inheritance from children's divorces, lawsuits and creditors, and keep the inheritance in the bloodline so it passes to grandchildren instead of to in-laws or strangers, Inheritance Trusts may be added as an option to either the RLT or the MAPT. These Inheritance Trusts are "stand-by trusts". They remain empty until the parent dies or, if there is a spouse, until the surviving spouse dies, and then the parents' trust or trusts pay out to the children's Inheritance Trusts.

2. Pour-Over Will

A new will which cancels your old will and provides that in case you may have left anything outside of your trust, the assets should be "poured into" your trust after you are gone, since your wishes are provided in the trust. Care should be taken to ensure that any assets left outside the trust are either joint with someone else or have a designated beneficiary. The use of the pour-over will is to be avoided, if possible, since it must be probated. It is there "just in case".

Examples of where a pour-over will might be used are (a) the client dies while waiting for an inheritance that is tied up in a probate proceeding, or (b) the client dies in a car accident and the estate comes into money damages.

3. Power of Attorney

Allows the person or persons you choose to handle your legal and financial affairs should you be unable to for any reason. There are distinct advantages to having an elder law estate planning attorney draft the power of attorney. Since they deal with disability on a daily basis, they are more aware of the essential powers that may be needed should a client become disabled. Some of the common powers that have been found useful to add to standard form powers are:

    a. To change beneficiaries on IRA's, annuities and insurance policies

    b. To create, fund or modify a trust

    c. To make gifts in unlimited amounts

These additional powers may make the difference between the client qualifying for Medicaid benefits one day or losing some or all of their assets.

4. Health Care Proxy/Living Will

The proxy is the person who you wish to make medical decisions for you if you are unable to decide for yourself. The living will authorizes termination of life support systems when your proxy determines that is best.

The general standard here is to withdraw life sustaining measures when the agent determines that the patient no longer has any meaningful existence and there is no hope of recovery. Nevertheless, it is important to note that the agent is carrying out the patient's express wishes, not those of the agent themselves.

5. Funeral and Burial Instructions

In your own handwriting you may provide:

    a. Type of funeral service

    b. Type of burial

    c. Whether funeral has been prepaid

    d. Who will be in charge of the arrangements

    e. What organs and tissues you may wish to donate

6. Final Instructions to Your Family

A form to fill out giving your family basic information they will need to settle your estate including:

    a. Date and place of any marriage

    b. Subscriptions that need to be cancelled

    c. Your computer user names and passwords

    d. Family, friends, businesses and professional advisors who should be contacted in the event of death

    e. Any information you would like included in your obituary

f. A checklist of what needs to be done by those settling your affairs, such as contacting Social Security and the Post Office

7. Deeds

New deeds should be prepared transferring your real property from your name into the name of your trust. This is important for out-of-state property as well to avoid "ancillary" probate in the other jurisdiction.

8. Memorandum of Personal Effects

Modern practice is to leave a handwritten list of which valuables go to which of the heirs and to request that the trustee honor the terms of the memorandum for those special items. This way, the client does not need to see the attorney to change their estate plan for personal effects. If they change their mind as to these personal items, they may simply tear up the old memorandum and write a new one.

9. Instructions for Transferring Assets to Your Trust

Although this is explained in person at the time the trust is executed, a written set of instructions will accompany the documents as well. Many law firms will undertake this exercise on your behalf, for an additional fee. However, most clients are able to do this for themselves.

10. Monitoring and Maintaining the Plan

At a minimum, a program should be in place to review the plan at least once every three years for changes in the law as well as in the client's assets, their health or in their personal lives and those of their heirs, such as births, death, marriages and divorces. This way, in the event of death or disability, which may occur many years later, the plan is always current. A law firm newsletter is also recommended to keep the client abreast of any law changes that may affect their plan on an ongoing basis.

6

Inheritance Trusts to Keep Assets in the Family

With the size of estates having grown today to where middle class families are leaving substantial bequests to their children (depending, of course, on how many children they have), the trend is toward establishing trusts for the children to keep the inheritance in the bloodline. In the case of your children, there are a number of benefits to leaving assets to them in a trust. These are: (1) the assets will be protected from claims by their spouse in the event of divorce (2) the assets may be protected from their creditors in the event of a lawsuit or other financial hardship, and (3) on your child's death, the unused assets will go to your blood relatives (usually grandchildren) instead of to in-laws or others.

We call this "multi-generational planning". Whereas with a will your estate plan usually dies when you do, with an Inheritance

Trust your wishes will go on for thirty, forty or even fifty or more years after you are gone, i.e., for two generations instead of just one.

These trusts provide that, during your children's lifetimes, they have complete access to the income and the principal of their Inheritance Trusts – so that you're not giving them a "gift with strings attached" or "ruling from the grave". But when your child dies, the Inheritance Trust which you have established directs that the remaining trust assets, which may have grown considerably, go to your grandchildren. If the grandchildren are under age thirty, we recommend that the funds be held in trust for them until such age, with the trustee (usually an aunt or uncle) using so much of the assets as may be needed for their health, education, maintenance and support. If one of your children dies without leaving children of their own, then the trust funds go to their surviving brothers and sisters.

Keep in mind that, without an Inheritance Trust, if your son or daughter dies, the entire inheritance you have left may go to a son-in-law or daughter-in-law who may later get remarried and share your hard earned assets with a complete stranger. Nevertheless, some clients would not want to completely leave out their son-in-law or daughter-in-law. In such cases, the Inheritance Trust, or a portion of it, such as one-half, may be set up to continue for your in-law's lifetime, providing them with the "income only" so that if they get remarried or end up in a nursing home, the assets are still protected. On their death the trust principal will then go to your grandchildren.

7

Special Needs Trusts for the Disabled Child or Grandchild

Parents or grandparents of a disabled child should leave assets in a Special Needs Trust, to avoid the child being disqualified from receiving government benefits, such as SSI and Medicaid. The reasoning behind these Special Needs Trusts is simple — prior to the protection now afforded by these trusts, parents would simply disinherit their disabled children rather than see them lose their benefits. Since the state wasn't getting the inheritance monies anyway, why not allow it to go to the disabled child for his or her extra needs, above and beyond what the state supplies, such as:

- Clothing

- Essential dietary needs

- Education

- Hobbies, sports, exercise

- Tickets for events

- Health care costs and medical procedures

- Vocational rehabilitation

- Household goods (appliances, furniture, computer, television)

- Personal care products

- Personal services (lawn mowing, housecleaning, babysitting, etc.)

- Music

- Real property

- Automobile (including gas and insurance)

- Transportation (buses, cabs, trains, domestic airfare)

- Vacations

- Burial costs

These trusts, however, offer traps for the unwary. Since payments to the child will generally reduce their SSI payments dollar for dollar, trustees of such trusts should be advised to make payments directly to the providers of goods and services. Preserving SSI benefits is crucial since eligibility for SSI determines eligibility for Medicaid.

In other words, if SSI is lost the recipient also loses their Medicaid benefits. In addition, any benefits previously paid by Medicaid may be recovered. As such, one also has to be mindful of bequests from well-meaning grandparents.

Distributions from the trust to the beneficiary should be "in kind" rather than in cash. For example, the trust may own items such as furniture and allow the beneficiary child the use of them. In addition, the Special Needs Trust must be carefully drafted so that it only allows payments for any benefits over and above what the government provides, not only now but also in the future. The child may not control or have direct access to any portion of the trust.

There are two types of Special Needs Trusts. First party and third party. The first party trust is set up by a parent, grandparent, legal guardian or court using the child's own money, either through earnings, an inheritance that was left directly to them or, perhaps, a personal injury award. These trusts require a "payback" provision, meaning that on the death of the child beneficiary, the trust must pay back the state for any government benefits received. In other words, the state is saying that, we will let you use this money for your special needs, but whatever was not needed should go back towards your basic care. These trusts require annual reporting and accounting to the state and are limited to children under age sixty-five.

A third party trust is usually set up by a parent or grandparent, using their own money. Here, no "payback" provision is required because it was not the child's own money that funded the trust and the parent or grandparent had no obligation to leave any assets to the child. Indeed, requiring a payback provision would discourage many parents from setting up a Special Needs Trust at all. Generally, on the death of the child beneficiary, the balance of the trust is paid out to the disabled child's children first, if any, otherwise to the surviving siblings, then nieces and nephews, etc.

A major issue for parents today is the increased life expectancy of their disabled child. With major advances in medical care, many disabled children, who would have in earlier days predeceased their parents, are now surviving them. In order to solve this problem, parents often leave a disproportionate share of the estate to the disabled child. This can engender hard feelings in siblings who, although agreeable to such an arrangement initially, may find themselves in need of funds later on and resentful of the uneven distribution in favor of the disabled child. The surviving siblings are often the only support network available for the special needs child so it is all the more important to keep peace and harmony in the family.

Often, an analysis with the elder law estate planning attorney will reveal that the assets from an equal division of the estate will, in fact, be sufficient to provide for the disabled child's needs. If such is not the case, "second-to-die" insurance may be purchased to provide for any additional funds needed. These policies are written over both parent's lives. Since the insurance company only has to pay when the second parent dies, the premiums are significantly lower than on a single life policy. Consideration should also be given to having the policy owned by an Irrevocable Life Insurance Trust (Chapter 15), for tax purposes.

Finally, in order to assist those who may have to care for the disabled child after the parent is gone, a "Letter of Intent" is often used. Here, the parent advises about any daily medical needs, their daily routines, their likes and dislikes, etc. Samples of the "Letter of Intent" for a special needs child are available on the Internet.

8

Second Marriage Planning

In second marriage planning, we sometimes recommend that the lawyer act as co-trustee on the death of the first spouse. While both spouses are living and competent they naturally run their trust or trusts together. But when one spouse dies, what prevents the other spouse from taking all of the assets and diverting them to their own children? Nothing at all, if they alone are in charge. While most people are honorable, and many are certain their spouse would never do such a thing, strange things often happen later in life. A spouse may become forgetful, delusional or senile or may be influenced, sometimes unduly, by other parties. Not only that, but what are the children of the deceased spouse going to feel when they find out their stepparent is in charge of all of the couple's assets? They often imagine the worst case scenario and feel very insecure and possibly even hostile to the surviving spouse.

As my esteemed trusts professor said to my law school class over forty years ago "you would be surprised at how fast the family glue comes undone."

Now, if you choose one of the deceased spouse's children to act as co-trustee with the surviving spouse what have you done? Created a potential minefield. The biggest issue is the conflict that exists whereby the stepchild may be reluctant to spend assets for the surviving spouse, because whatever is spent on him or her will come out of that child's inheritance. Then what if stepparent gets remarried? How will the stephchild trustee react to that event? What if it turns out the stepchild liked the stepparent when his parent was living and married to him or her, but not so much or not at all afterwards?

Here is where the lawyer as trustee may provide an ideal solution. When parent dies, the lawyer steps in as co-trustee with the surviving spouse. The lawyer helps the stepparent to invest for their own benefit as well as making sure the principal grows to offset inflation, for the benefit of the heirs.

It is a firmly established legal principal that there is no ethical prohibition against the attorney recommending himself to act as a trustee on behalf of a client or client's estate. And for good reason. In many situations the counselor may provide invaluable assistance that no one else is willing or able to provide.

The stepparent in this case takes care of all their business privately with their lawyer. The trusts cannot be raided. These protections may also be extended for IRA and 401(k) money passing to the spouse through the use of the "IRA Contract". Surviving spouse agrees ahead of time that they will make an irrevocable designation of the deceased spouse's children as beneficiaries when the IRA is left to the surviving spouse, and further agrees that any withdrawals in excess of the required minimum distribution (RMD) may only be made on consent of the lawyer.

What about the deceased spouse's children? When the trust terms are read they will feel very secure that the lawyer their father chose will continue on for the stepparent's lifetime, looking after and protecting their share of the assets. They are relieved by the protection that has been set up for them, have no animosity or concern about the stepparent's having sole control of the assets and the relationship between the families may continue smoothly and even grow and flourish.

10

Planning for Singles and Couples Without Children

For singles and couples without children, the lawyer as co-trustee fulfills an entirely different function. In the couples setting, we are referring to the issues that arise after the first spouse dies. From an estate planning point of view, couples without children ultimately have the same issues as singles.

So whether you are single now or become one after your partner dies, your key issue is usually not planning for death, not who you are leaving it to and certainly not having a will. Your key issue is planning for disability. Should you be unable, at some point, to handle your financial and legal affairs due to accident or illness, who will take over? If you don't have a strong plan for disability, which eventually happens to about half of all people, you are at considerable risk of having the wrong person or a stranger take over your affairs. In the event of disability, virtually any interested party (hospital, doctor, lawyer, social worker, relative, etc.) may initiate a proceeding to have a legal guardian appointed for you. Once you enter into this bureaucratic process, usually involuntarily, it is difficult to extricate yourself and you lose precious control over your affairs. We often say you are only as strong as your back-up plan. If you have set up a living trust, you put yourself in charge now, but the trust says who takes over in the event of disability. You get the person or persons you have chosen, not a court appointed legal guardian, along with the thousands of dollars in costs that such proceedings entail.

So, who should you choose? We recommend that you choose two people. One a friend or relative who is willing to undertake the responsibility and then the lawyer as co-trustee. The lawyer will see to it that the trust is run properly and that all of your affairs are handled according to law. It takes a considerable amount of the anxiety, pressure and responsibility off of your friend or relative who has so kindly agreed to undertake this task. Further, you have two people signing off on all decisions, and everyone knows what two heads are better than. Not only is the possibility of a mistake being made greatly reduced, but it also eliminates the risk of misappropriation of assets. We are also mindful that one person, acting alone, may be influenced by someone else who you didn't choose.

In some cases, where clients do not have a friend or relative available for this purpose or where they do not want to burden anyone with the responsibility, the lawyer may act as sole trustee.

In our view, planning for disability is more important than planning for death. In the case of disability, the lawyer as co-trustee may be an invaluable asset to the person without immediate family.

10

Protecting Assets for Spendthrift Children

It's an estate planning epidemic. So many successful parents we meet have children who are poor at handling money, have not achieved significant success in life where they have any experience in handling money, or they simply refuse to grow up. What's a parent to do?

Enter what has been termed the greatest invention of English common law: the trust. Trusts are legal entities that may hold and use assets for a beneficiary (your son or daughter) but have them managed by a trustee (one of more responsible adults, including a professional trustee).

Historically, estate planning consisted of setting up a will and leaving everything to one's children in equal shares, "per stirpes".

The "per stirpes" is Latin for "by the roots", meaning that if any of the children predecease their parents then their share goes to their children, if any.

Today, however, adolescence lasts much longer than it used to. Some say that "30 is the new 20" and, anecdotally, we see much evidence of this. Another recent phenomenon is children coming back home to live with their parents, for many reasons, but often having to do with their inability to deal with the problems of life or the shrunken job market.

In light of the foregoing, and the fact that trusts, which have become as common as wills today, may continue for many years after the death of the parent, new planning options are available to clients.

For example, one popular plan of distribution is 20% at age thirty, one-half of the remaining balance at thirty-five and the remainder at forty. The theory here is that the child can get the 20% and spend it all, but they have to wait five years before they get one-half of what's left and then, finally, ten years later, when they have hopefully made their mistakes and matured somewhat, they still have about one-half of the inheritance left. A twist on this plan is 20% on the death of the parent, one-half of the remaining balance five years after the parent's death and the remainder ten years after the parent's death. This latter formula is often accompanied by a "cap". For example, upon attaining the age of fifty, any undistributed amounts shall then be distributed outright to the adult child beneficiary.

It is important to note here that assets left in the trust for delayed distribution are still available for the child's health, education, maintenance and support. Those assets are simply managed by the more experienced and mature trustee who makes decisions as to distribution of income and principal.

What if the parent wishes to "rule from the grave" and keep the assets in trust for the child's lifetime?

Let's say your son Richard is a problem. Your estate plan using a living trust would provide that upon your death or, if you have a spouse, upon the second death, Richard's share would go into The Richard Trust with perhaps a family member and your attorney as co-trustees. The Richard Trust would continue for his lifetime, and the trustees use the money for Richard's health, education, maintenance and support. The trust may help him start a business, buy a house or, alternatively, purchase a house for him. Then, upon his death, the trust would go to his children (at a stated age).

The "sprinkling", or "spray" trust is also often used in this context. Let's say Richard has two children and you are very concerned about them as well. You may set up a trust for Richard and his children and direct the trustee to "sprinkle" the income and principal amongst the beneficiaries, in equal or unequal amounts, whenever it is needed or will do the most good. So if one of Richard's children is accepted to Harvard, while the other goes to the local community college, the trust may help both. An added bonus with these trusts is that they keep the assets out of the hands of Richard's spouse who, in some cases, may be a large part of the financial problem.

For children in dire financial straits or perhaps headed in that general direction, the effects of a potential bankruptcy on the inheritance and estate administration must be addressed. What happens if your son or daughter files for bankruptcy within six months of the date of your death? The inherited assets are then available for their creditors. Nevertheless, by leaving assets to your son or daughter in a trust, giving the trustee discretion to distribute income and principal as the trustee sees fit, you may protect those assets from being lost in a subsequent bankruptcy proceeding.

There is much to consider concerning setting up a trust for an adult child, such as the pros and cons of naming siblings, other relatives, friends and professional advisors as trustees. Other factors are how long the trust should go on, what payments the trust should allow or disallow, and who the back-up trustees might be. All your choices have their issues which need to be fleshed out, with the help of an experienced attorney, so as to provide the plan that best suits your family's needs.

11

Planning for
Same Sex Couples

Same sex couples face unique estate planning issues since, in many jurisdictions, their unions are not legally protected. Living trusts are often the estate planning vehicle of choice for the gay community for a number of reasons.

1. They provide for your partner to be able to handle your assets should you become disabled. Powers of attorney and health care proxies/living wills are ancillary documents that also help insure that your partner will be in charge of all legal, financial and medical decision-making in the event of disability, free of interference from other family members.

2. Will planning has fallen into disfavor because (a) wills are significantly easier to challenge than trusts (b) a notice of the

proceeding must be given to your closest legal heirs, providing them with an opportunity to object (c) the will is a public record, eliminating privacy, and (d) the legal process may be time consuming, possibly delaying the surviving partner's access to needed funds.

3. Simply putting your partner's name on your assets, or joint tenancy, seems to be a simple solution to many, until they learn of the pitfalls. First, for appreciated assets, such as stocks and real estate, there are tax disadvantages to receiving assets from a joint tenant. While inheriting from a will or trust at death eliminates taxable capital gains for the survivor, joint tenancy only eliminates one-half of those capital gains since you are only "inheriting" one-half of the property. Secondly, you may be exposed to the debts and liabilities of your partner. Thirdly, you lose control over where the assets go after your surviving partner dies. Perhaps you may want to provide for your partner for life, but state where the unused assets will go after he or she passes. Finally, once you make your assets joint with your partner, you may have more difficulty in getting those assets back in the event of a break up in the relationship.

4. If either or both partners have children, care must be taken as to how those children are provided for on the death of the first partner. Many of the same considerations apply as in second marriage planning (Chapter 7), such as what they will receive when their parent dies and what they will receive when the surviving partner dies, as well as how their rights will be protected in the interim.

5. Funeral and burial arrangements are often contentious matters. Proper legal documents will allow you to designate the person you

wish to have control of the arrangements as well as providing in writing the specific type of funeral and burial that you may wish.

6. As same sex couples age, there may be good reasons not to marry for Medicaid planning purposes. Whereas for married couples the combined assets of the couple are available for the care of the ill spouse, such is not the case for unmarried couples. So your assets are legally protected from your partner's cost of care. Further, while married couples who wish to plan ahead five years by setting up a Medicaid Asset Protection Trust (MAPT) may not name each other as trustee, such is not the case for unmarried couples. So if you wish to protect your home and life savings from nursing home costs, and cannot obtain long-term care insurance for any reason, you may each establish MAPT's for each other and need not go outside the relationship to put someone else in charge in order to protect your assets.

In our experience, crafting an estate plan for the same sex couple that is thought through, addressing all the potential social, legal, financial, health and tax issues, is a loving act that provides peace of mind knowing your choices will be legally protected and honored.

12

Elder Law Estate Planning Issues for Women

When Husband Handled the Finances

While women and men have many issues in common, some of these issues tend to affect women more deeply. For example, in the case of the death or disability of a spouse, it is more often the surviving wife who is unfamiliar with handling the family finances. In the course of planning for such a couple, it is wise to find a financial advisor that the wife can turn to. Ideally, this relationship should be developed over the years while the husband is living, so that there is a seamless transfer of decision-making. Where such a relationship with a financial advisor is absent, one of the financially savvy children may be named as a co-trustee with the surviving wife or, should none of the children be suitable for that role, the attorney as co-trustee may be considered.

Children from Prior Marriages

With the increase in second marriages, many women have children from previous marriages. How will those children fare should a wife die first? This dynamic may be complicated by the fact that there are children from the second marriage as well as the first. Here, we consider making partial gifts to the children of the first marriage, who are generally older, on the wife's death. The balance of the assets may be kept in trust for the surviving husband, providing for him during his lifetime and, on his death, paying out to the wife's children from the second marriage. Alternatively, wife's entire estate may be held in trust and pay out to all of her children in equal shares after the husband dies.

In the second marriage context, what about the husband's children from a prior marriage? If the wife is going to be financially dependent on some or all of his assets after his death, she may want to avoid the situation when one or more of the husband's children are in charge of the money after he dies. Here, the pitfalls are many. They may not wish to distribute principal to her, feeling that the funds are coming out of their inheritance. She may find out that they do not care for her personally, even though this was not apparent when their father was alive. They may disapprove of her subsequent remarriage. We have recommended to many women clients that they choose the lawyer to act as co-trustee with her after a husband's death. This way, the conflict of interest that the husband's children have is eliminated and she may handle her personal and financial business privately with her own lawyer. Second marriage planning, more fully discussed in Chapter 8, is particularly important for women.

Medicaid Issues for Women

Since women tend to live longer than men, they make up the majority of nursing home residents. Planning to protect assets, especially the family's home, from being lost to the costs of long-term care, is essential. Medicaid Asset Protection Trusts (MAPT's) should be into place when a husband dies. While the home was exempt from Medicaid when the spouse was living, it becomes an available resource, required to be "spent down" if a single person requires long-term care.

What if it is a second marriage and the couple has executed a pre-nuptial agreement? Many are surprised to learn that they are financially responsible for the cost of their husband's care despite the prenuptial agreement. Medicaid is not bound by that agreement and considers the combined assets of the couple to be available for the care of the ill spouse, regardless of whose name those assets are in. Before contemplating a second marriage later in life, especially where the man is older, a woman should determine whether her intended has long-term care insurance or, if not, is willing and able to purchase that insurance so that her assets are protected. If he is unable or unwilling to purchase long-term care insurance, she should consider setting up a MAPT for herself to protect her assets.

Women's Role as Caregivers

Fair or not, women tend to care for their aging parents far more often than men. What if a woman has to take unpaid leave from employment for this purpose? Caregiver Agreements (Chapter 19) are designed to compensate the daughter for the job of caring and sometimes boarding her aging parents. Consideration should be given to having siblings agree to the terms of the Caregiving Agreement to avoid misunderstandings later on. There may be the need for a "lump-sum" distribution to the daughter to improve her home or put an addition on for the parents to reside in. The parents may wish to acquire life rights to stay in that home in exchange for the lump sum payment. Discussion should occur as to whether some or all of the lump sum will be considered a gift to be subtracted out of the daughter's ultimate share of the inheritance.

Where the responsibility lies with the daughter caregiver, we recommend that she be named as the agent under the parent's power of attorney as well as the agent for medical decisions under the health care proxy and/or living will. Wherever possible, we advise against these powers residing with a sibling who lives far away. It is difficult for the daughter who bears the bulk of the responsibility not to have the powers to adequately discharge that responsibility, not to mention the annoyance of being second-guessed by a sibling who is not there day-to-day to see what is going on.

Medicaid Asset Protection Trust (MAPT) planning (Chapter 20) should also be considered for the parents at this time. Even the strongest and most well intentioned caregiver may ultimately find themselves overwhelmed and unable to cope with the burden of caregiving. Other risks for the caregiver may be (1) a health issue or other crisis that arises for her or a member of her family, or (2) the parent requiring a level of skilled care that is beyond the daughter's ability to provide. In the foregoing situations, a nursing home stay may become inevitable. The daughter should take all steps from the very beginning to protect assets since, being in charge, she will later be answerable to her siblings for the actions she may or may not have taken. Here, reliance on the elder law attorney's advice may well insulate from later claims.

13

Disclaimer Trusts for Couples with Taxable Estates

For couples with taxable estates, disclaimer trusts are commonly used today to allow the surviving spouse greater flexibility in optimizing estate tax savings. These trusts are generally used in states that have a "state" estate tax that the client my be exposed to.

Here's how they work. Each spouse sets up their revocable living trust. Husband and wife are co-trustees of his trust, using his social security number and, similarly, they are both co-trustees of her trust with her social security number. Let's say husband dies first. His trust says "leave everything to my wife except that, whatever she disclaims, i.e. refuses to take, will remain in my trust". The disclaimer is a legal document that lists the assets disclaimed and their value. Wife remains as trustee on husband's trust after he dies and may use the funds in his trust for her health, maintenance and support. She may also remove 5% of the trust every year for any reason or $5,000, whichever is greater.

The reason wife is limited to health, maintenance and support is that if she had the right to take whatever she wanted at any time for any reason, the IRS would say that she had complete control of the funds and would then seek to tax those funds in her estate. The access for health, maintenance and support, however, is sufficiently broad so as not to cause a problem for her. She may also continue to buy, sell and trade assets in the husband's trust. This trust continues for her lifetime and pays out to the heirs at her death along with her own trust.

Husband's social security number died with him so his trust took out a trust tax identification number when he died and reported as a separate taxpayer during her lifetime. It is not includable in her estate. Indeed, what has happened is that husband's trust was settled on his death and left to his heirs, but subject to wife's lifetime use and enjoyment of the trust assets.

The benefit of the disclaimer is that it allows the wife to decide (or the husband if wife dies first) how much to leave in the deceased spouse's trust based on her age, health and the tax laws at that future time. Formerly, attorneys would simply do their best to split the assets between the two trusts and simply say whatever was in the deceased spouse's trust remained there for the surviving spouse's lifetime. This yielded some unfortunate results.

Let's say husband's trust exceeds the tax exempt amount. Formerly, wife would be required to pay tens of thousands of dollars in state estate tax based on the amount over the exemption. With the disclaimer trust, wife may take the excess over the exemption out of his trust for herself and claim the unlimited marital deduction which avoids estate tax on assets left to a spouse. Perhaps her estate will be under the exemption and no taxes will ever have to be paid on that money, she may spend or gift it down, or the exemption may be raised during her lifetime. In any event, worst case scenario is that taxes on those monies are deferred until after she dies and, in the meantime, she has the use and enjoyment of monies that would have formerly gone to the government.

A word about the Federal estate tax exemption which today exceeds five million dollars. For couples over five million, the Federal tax regime offer "portability" which means the surviving spouse is permitted to claim any unused portion of the deceased spouse's exemption. Nevertheless, the disclaimer trust may still be used to "freeze" the growth of the deceased spouse's share.

For example, let's say husband's trust has five million dollars. If it goes to wife, she can claim his five million plus exemption (adjusted for inflation) on her death. However, the five million may have grown to ten million by the time of her death which, together with her own assets, may put her estate over the combined ten million plus exemption.

Be leaving the five million in husband's trust at his death, all of the growth remains tax-free to the children at the wife's death. The husband's trust has passed the tax collector and is not looked at again upon the wife's death.

At an estate tax rate of forty percent, millions of dollars may be saved at the Federal estate tax level by using disclaimer trusts.

14

The Irrevocable
Life Insurance Trust (ILIT)

M any clients are surprised to learn that the death proceeds of their life insurance are subject to estate taxation. They believe that life insurance escapes estate taxes and passes to their loved ones intact.

This confusion probably began when the client was told that life insurance is <u>income tax-free</u>. For married clients, the confusion is compounded by the belief that the unlimited marital deduction somehow magically insulates the client's death proceeds from ever being taxed. Often the marital deduction merely postpones the heavy tax burden on such death proceeds until the second spouse dies.

For clients who have taxable estates, estate taxes may consume up to forty percent of their life insurance proceeds.

These clients actually have far less insurance than they think they have or, alternatively, they are paying far more for their coverage than they should be paying.

The proceeds from your life insurance are generally includable in your taxable estate if you owned the policy or had any "incidents of ownership." This is true for term insurance, cash value insurance, and even insurance provided by your employer.

"Incidents of ownership" which will cause life insurance death proceeds to be taxed as part of the insured's taxable estate include not just policy ownership, but also the right to borrow the cash value, the right to change beneficiaries, and the right to change how the proceeds are ultimately distributed to the beneficiaries.

The Irrevocable Life Insurance Trust (or "ILIT" as it is frequently called) has proven to be a highly effective method of avoiding estate taxes without the many problems of transferring ownership of the policy to the client's children or other heirs (as discussed more fully below).

An ILIT is created to own one or more policies insuring your life. The ILIT is irrevocable, meaning you cannot generally change the terms once it has been signed. You must also choose someone else as trustee of the ILIT besides you and your spouse (a knowledgeable professional is the ideal choice).

You cannot be a beneficiary of the trust, but your children may be (and usually are) beneficiaries. Quite often, the ILIT parallels the dispositive provisions of your revocable living trust or other estate planning documents, although there is no legal requirement for the ILIT to do so.

Moreover, the ILIT cannot be payable to your estate or to your revocable living trust, as this would bring the policy proceeds back into your taxable estate.

Your contribution to the ILIT represents gifts which you cannot get back. The gifts are usually used to pay the premiums on one or more policies insuring your life and which are owned by the trust. Because you cannot reclaim the policies, or receive any benefit from the trust, it would be inappropriate to have the trust own policies whose cash values you had planned to use for retirement income.

Currently, you may gift up to $14,000 per year per donee (recipient) without any gift tax implications. This exclusion is only available to gifts of a present interest, which is something you may enjoy or use now, and gifts in trust generally do not qualify, as they are gifts of a future interest, or one that will be enjoyed or used later. You may exceed the $14,000 year limitation by filing a Federal gift tax return and using some of your five million plus estate tax exemption to exempt the lifetime gift. In other words, the amounts you give that exceed the $14,000 are simply subtracted from the five million plus you can give at death.

To avoid the gift being considered a prohibited gift of a future interest, your ILIT should provide that each lifetime beneficiary (who must also be beneficiary or contingent beneficiary at your death) has the right to withdraw his or her proportionate share of the contribution for a limited period of time after each contribution is made.

Usually the trust agreement provides that, after a contribution is made, each beneficiary will be notified of their right of withdrawal. After the expiration of the withdrawal period (usually not less than 30 days), the trustee may use the contribution to pay the premium on a life insurance policy.

The IRS has approved the ILIT concept when all the technical requirements are met, but the IRS is known for challenging ILITs when the requirements are not met. Even the order in which the documents are signed may be critical.

Existing policies may be transferred to your ILIT, but the death proceeds will be drawn back into your taxable estate if you die within three years of completing this gift. Also, the transfer of existing policies may trigger a taxable event. If you are insurable, it is sometimes advisable to consider a new policy.

The trustee receives the death benefit upon your death. These proceeds may be distributed to your family, held in trust, or used to purchase assets from your estate or from your revocable living trust. This last option would be important if your estate had insufficient liquid assets to pay estate taxes.

The tax on your estate is due nine months after the date of death. Those with large estates often do not have sufficient cash or other assets which could be easily converted to cash within the nine month time frame. The need to pay estate taxes has caused many a farm, family business, or major real estate holding to be sold at discounted prices to pay the estate tax.

Life insurance may provide the money needed to pay the estate tax, and by having the policy purchased and held in an ILIT, the proceeds may be used to provide the needed liquidity for your estate and yet not be subject to estate tax on your death.

Married couples may wish to consider using a "second-to-die" or "survivorship life" policy which pays the death benefit only after both spouses are deceased. That is usually the exact time that the proceeds are needed to pay the estate taxes since it is relatively easy to plan to avoid all estate taxes on the death of the first spouse, through the use of the unlimited marital deduction. Because no death benefit is paid on the first death, the premium is much lower than purchasing a policy which insures just one life.

Often clients try to accomplish similar results to the ILIT by having, say, their two children own the policy equally. Many problems may arise under such an arrangement. A child may predecease the parent; the policy may be attached and liquidated by a child's creditors; the policy may be considered as the child's property in the event of a divorce; one child may refuse to pay the premiums or may wish to borrow the cash value, etc. The outright gift of a policy makes no provisions for your children or grandchildren other than payment of proceeds. For example, you may want to provide that the proceeds be made payable to their Inheritance Trusts (Chapter 6). These and other issues may be addressed in a properly drafted ILIT.

If you have a taxable estate and own a large insurance policy, or are contemplating purchasing one, you would be well advised to consider how the ILIT might benefit you and your family.

15

Writing an Ethical Will –
Legacy Development

Bequeathing Who You Are and What You Stand For

In the course of preparing this chapter I mentioned to a client that I would be writing about ethical wills, "I thought all your wills were ethical," he deadpanned.

While a legal will bequeaths valuables, an ethical will bequeaths values, such as how to lead a moral and upright life. Questions of the heart and soul may creep in as we age – have I fulfilled my purpose? What will I be remembered for? What kind of legacy have I passed on to my family and others?

While not legally binding, ethical wills are excellent vehicles for clarifying and communicating the meaning of our lives to our families. Those who want to be remembered authentically and for their gifts of heart, mind and spirit, can take satisfaction in knowing what they hold most valued is "on the record," not to be lost or forgotten. Imagine the richness that might be added to our lives if we had a legacy such as this from our grandparents or our great-grandparents of whom many of us know little if anything at all.

An early example of an ethical will occurs in Shakespeare's Hamlet where Polonius advises his son, Laertes:

> *"Give every man thy ear, but few thy voice,*
> *Take each man's censure, but reserve thy judgement...*
> *Neither a borrower not a lender (be),*
> *For (loan) oft loses both itself and friend...*
> *This above all: to thine own self be true,*
> *and it must follow, as the night the day,*
> *Thou canst not then be false of any man."*

In ancient times, most people had little opportunity to control the distribution of their property (assuming they owned any); however, they were free to speak their minds as it related to the disposition of "moral" assets. Ethical wills were particularly advantageous outlets for women, since society's rules usually precluded them from writing a legal will or dispensing property as they wished. Historians have found examples of ethical wills authored by women during the medieval period, usually in the form of letters or books written to the children.

People usually associate the term "will" with "after death." Legal wills are read after death. At one time ethical wills were passed on and read after death as well; however, that's less often the case today. A living will, on the other hand, is a document that contains specific instructions about medically related issues, meant to be followed while the person is still alive but unable to communicate his or her wishes directly at the time these decision points are reached.

What all three types of wills have in common is the fact that they provide instructions to others as to the intentions of the author. When considering what you might include in your ethical will it may be productive to consider your past, present and future. Some of our values and beliefs have been passed on to us from our predecessors. Our own life experiences shape our character and help form a foundation of our values and principles. Looking into the future we might ponder what we may yet come to and what we have left to do.

Common Themes in Ethical Wills

Common themes from our past:

Meaningful personal or family stories

Lessons learned from personal or familial experience

Regrets

Common themes from the present:

Personal values and beliefs

Values and beliefs of the author's faith community

Expressions of love and gratitude

Apologies

Common themes from the future:

Blessings, dreams, and hopes for present and future generations

Advice and guidance

Requests

Funeral plans

Creating an ethical will is a way to:

Learn about myself

Reflect on my life

Affirm myself

An ethical will is a forum in which to:

Fill in knowledge gaps of will recipients by providing historic or ancestral information that links generations

Convey feelings, thoughts, and "truths", that are hard to say face-to-face

Express regrets and apologies

Open the door to forgiving and being forgiven

Come to terms with my mortality

Writing an ethical will may be:

A spiritual experience that provides a sense of completion to my life

A loving undertaking that helps my loved ones "let go" when my time comes

16

Ten Reasons
to Plan Your Estate

1. Makes sure your estate goes to whom you want, when you want, the way you want. Most estate plans, be they wills or trusts, leave the assets to the next generation outright (i.e., in their hands) in equal shares. However, with a little bit of thought on your part, and some guidance from an experienced elder law estate planning attorney, you may dramatically improve the way your estate is ultimately distributed. For example, you may delay large bequests until children or grandchildren are older or give it to them in stages so that they have the chance to make some mistakes with the money without jeopardizing the whole inheritance. Similarly, you may place conditions on receipt of the money such as "only upon graduation with a bachelor's degree" or "only to be used to purchase an annuity to provide a lifetime income for the beneficiary". The possibilities, of course, are endless. The point here is that if you have some issue with one of your beneficiaries, talk it over with your attorney and you might be pleasantly surprised with some of the suggestions he or she may have for you.

2. Allows you to give back to the people and places that have helped you. Again, most people leave their assets to their children in equal shares. Yet time and again we see children who really don't need the money or, unfortunately, don't deserve it. Even when they do need and deserve it, there is a place for remembering those people and institutions who have helped make you what you are today. There is much good that is done through local community foundations if you want to show your appreciation for what your community has done for you. Think of the benefits you have garnered over your lifetime from your alma mater or the depth and richness added to your life by your place of worship. These can be some of the most satisfying gifts you will ever make.

3. It proves stewardship by showing your family that you cared enough to plan for them. When you put time, thought and effort into planning your affairs it sends a powerful message to your loved ones. You are saying that you handled the matter with care and diligence. This will reflect itself in how the money is received, invested and spent by your heirs. If you took it seriously, it is much more likely they will handle it well themselves, including seeing to it that their affairs are properly planned.

4. Saves your heirs legal fees, taxes and time in settling your affairs. Everyone understands and wants to save fees and taxes, but what about saving time? By planning ahead with trusts instead of wills, you may abbreviate the settlement process, thus aiding the grieving process by allowing families to heal more quickly and get on with their lives. In addition, while assets are tied up in a lengthy estate proceeding, valuable opportunities may be lost or additional expenses incurred, such as having to maintain a home. With the volatility of investments today, no one can afford to have their affairs tied up for any significant amount of time.

5. Protects your assets from being eaten up by nursing home costs. No estate plan is complete without a plan to protect it from having to "spend down" your assets if you have to go into a nursing home. Here, you may be advised on long-term care insurance or, if you don't qualify due to medical or economic reasons, you may be looking at alternatives such as setting up trusts to protect your assets from nursing home costs or transferring assets to other family members for safekeeping. Does your estate plan have some form of nursing home protection?

6. Allows you to continue your IRA's for generations. IRA rules allow you to multiply your IRA three to ten times or more by "stretching" them out for your children or grandchildren. When a parent dies and leaves an IRA to a child, the child may not roll over the IRA into their own, but instead must take a distribution. However, with proper advice, your son or daughter may elect under the Internal Revenue Code to take the distribution out in small increments over their lifetime. For example, if son is age thirty when parent dies, he has a 52 year remaining life expectancy. If he elects for the "stretch-out", he takes 1/52nd the year after the parent died, then 1/51st the following year, etc. This is also known as an "Inherited IRA".

7. Allows you to protect the inheritance from children's divorces, lawsuits. With middle class people often leaving hundreds of thousands of dollars to their children, doesn't it make sense to protect the inheritance from the high rate of divorce? By leaving assets to your children in an Inheritance Trust, you may not only protect it from a divorce but, in many cases, also from creditors in the event your son or daughter ever gets sued. This means that their money may be protected (1) if they or someone they are legally responsible for ever has a major medical problem (2) if they get sued for a personal injury claim (3) if they lose their job or business and have to file for bankruptcy, etc.

8. Makes sure your estate will pass by blood instead of by marriage. Most estate plans leave the money to the children. So let's say that you have left $250,000 to your son and $250,000 to your daughter. Now if they die (remember this is after you're gone) who inherits from them? Your son-in-law or daughter-in-law. Can they get remarried and share your $250,000 with a complete stranger? Sure. Happens all the time. What can you do about it? By leaving your assets in an Inheritance Trust for your children, you can give them complete control over their inheritance (so you're not "ruling from the grave") while at the same time providing that, when they die, whatever they didn't spend goes to your grandchildren or your other surviving children, instead of to your in-laws.

9. Guarantees you will be protected if you become disabled. About half of all people today have a period of disability before they die. Without a plan, you risk getting the state's plan where they appoint a legal guardian for you who (1) may be someone you don't even know (2) may change your investments (3) may be unable to protect your assets by transferring them to other family members if you have to go into a nursing home, and (4) may make it difficult to get back control of your assets if you recover from your disability. When you set up a revocable living trust, you create a plan for disability that avoids a guardianship proceeding, puts the persons you choose in control and allows them to transfer and protect assets. Again, with the high rate of disability later in life, we all need to plan for it.

10. It gives you peace of mind so that you can get on with your life. When you have a well thought out and executed plan you actually feel better. You feel safe and secure that no matter what happens you have a plan to deal with it and you have your team in place to carry it out. This allows you to put those concerns out of your mind and get on with the business of enjoying your life.

17

Business Succession Planning

While ninety percent of American businesses are family owned, only about thirty percent of them continue to the next generation. Half of those again make it to the third generation. The most common reason: lack of a business succession plan.

There are many reasons owners fail to plan. In addition to confronting the issues of age and mortality, the business owner also faces potentially giving up his or her life's work – often a venture started, nurtured and grown by him or her over many years.

Business succession planning should start while the entrepreneur is young enough to spend time monitoring the next generation, be it family or otherwise. Around the age of sixty should allow enough time, say five to ten years, for the process to begin and develop.

One of the first things the owner should consider is what to do with the new found time as others take on more of the burden of running the business. Other goals to achieve will help the principal transition to a new life that does not center around the former work and lifestyle.

A business plan should be created, or an existing one modified, to take into account the reality of the succession, ideally with input from the successors. This will allow for the personal feelings, ambitions and goals of everyone concerned to be accounted for. Professional advisors will need to be consulted – accountants for business evaluations and tax planning, lawyers for estate planning and to prepare agreements and financial advisors to determine investment and income strategies for the departing owner and their spouse.

Two of the methods used to transfer ownership are as follows:

1. Gifting using the annual exclusion. Currently at $14,000 per year and indexed to inflation, a couple who files a joint tax return may annually elect to "split" the gift and give $28,000 worth of stock in the company to each child (or any other person for that matter). In addition to the annual exclusion, each spouse may gift about five million dollars over their lifetimes. A gift tax return must be filed but no tax is due since the client is merely using a portion of their estate tax exemption during their lifetime. So, for example, if you gift out $1,000,000 today, you only have $4,000,000 left to

gift tax-free upon your death. If you feel the business is going to appreciate rapidly in the future, now might be a good time to use some or all of the lifetime gift tax exemption to get the business, or property owned by it, out of your estate, to avoid potentially heavy estate taxes later.

If the owner feels that the successors may not be ready to receive substantial portions of the business, but still wishes to move assets out of their name now for tax purposes, irrevocable trusts may be used. These trusts may then further transfer assets to the successors at a time or series of times in the future.

2. The major tool used in effectuating a business-succession plan is the "buy-sell agreement". The buy-sell agreement stipulates that the seller must sell and the buyer must buy, at a pre-determined value (adjust from time to time between the parties), and upon a predetermined event. Events triggering the provisions of the agreement include, but are not limited to, retirement, disability or death.

There are many forms of buy-sell agreements. The most common is the cross-purchase agreement whereby the remaining shareholders or partners, as the case may be, agree to purchase the departing owner's share of the enterprise upon retirement, disability or death. The agreement is typically funded with insurance for death or disability but, for retirement, the remaining owners will typically have to fund the agreement through the profits of the business. Upon death, the insurance may still be used to confer a remaining benefit on the departing owner's heirs. The retiring owner's retirement income interest may be secured with a private annuity or a promissory note executed by the business itself and perhaps personally guaranteed as well. The foregoing strategies may also include survivor's benefits for the owner's spouse.

In cases where there are no other shareholders or partners, key employees should be considered as potential buyers under the agreement since they will best be able to run the business and generate the income needed to fund the owner's retirement and/or pay the insurance premiums.

With the right amount of thought and expertise brought to bear on the problem of succession, the business will more likely be one of the few that confers benefits on the owner's family for generations to come – leaving a lasting legacy to his or her dedication, hard work and foresight.

18

Prenuptial Agreements

Prenuptial agreements ("prenups") are contracts entered into by a couple before marriage setting out the rights of the parties in the event of divorce or death. Less common is the postnuptial agreement, with similar terms, but executed by the parties after marriage.

Who signs these types of agreements and why? Often couples marrying for the second or more time will have children and/or substantial assets at the time of remarriage. They may wish to insure that all or some of their assets go to their children and not to the new spouse, who may have children and assets of their own. Even with a will which leaves everything to one's children, without a prenup the surviving spouse is legally entitled to claim about half of the deceased spouse's estate. Having been married before, these couples know that sometimes things do not work out and wish to simplify matters in the event of a divorce, including whether or not alimony will be payable.

In the prenup there must be full disclosure so that each party knows what they are giving up. A necessary component is a schedule whereby each party sets out a list of their separate property, i.e. what they owned prior to entering into the marriage. The agreement then sets out the division of property in the event of divorce as well as the inheritance rights between the parties. While prenups often provide that neither party will inherit from the other, it is not unusual for the parties to partially waive those provisions after a few years and execute a will or trust leaving assets to the spouse despite the prenup. Other ways to leave assets to the spouse are by making some assets joint or naming the spouse as beneficiary on IRA's, investments, bank accounts, annuities or insurance policies. The prenup may also contain a "sunset provision" that it expires after the parties have been married for a set number of years.

When there is great economic disparity between the parties, or one of them owns a business, the wealthy spouse may want to protect themselves (as Donald Trump is well known to have done) and, similarly, the less well off spouse will want to establish what they will receive in assets and/or alimony in the event of divorce. If there are business partners of one of the spouses, they may want protection so that the new spouse does not become a partner in the business by way of inheritance.

In our experience, prenups do not work well with younger couples about to enter into a first marriage. They are considered unromantic and usually the young couple does not have sufficient assets to be concerned. While some of them may be coming into substantial inheritances, the invention of the Inheritance Trust has solved this problem. Parents may now leave the inheritance to a trust that protects the assets for their son or daughter in the event of divorce and pass it by blood, instead of by marriage. In the event of death, the child's spouse has no right to make a claim against a trust set up by a third party.

Medicaid Planning Strategies

19

Protecting Assets With Caregiver Agreements

Family members as caregivers overwhelmingly provide for elderly and disabled loved ones at home. Although a labor of love, taking care of ailing loved ones also has a market value, meaning that caretakers may be paid as a way to protect assets.

Through the use of a Caregiver Agreement, also known as a Personal Services Contract, the disabled or elderly person may transfer money to family members as compensation rather than as a gift. Gifts to family members made in the last five years before applying for Medicaid to pay for nursing home costs disqualify the applicant from receiving Medicaid for a certain period of time, known as a "penalty period."

For example, mom depends on daughter Janice for her care. If mom gifts $100,000 to Janice, then goes into a nursing home in the next five years and applies for Medicaid, the gift to Janice will result in about a ten month penalty period. Janice will have to give the $100,000 back to mom to pay nursing home costs during the penalty period, or mom will have to use other resources to pay.

Instead, using a Caregiver Agreement, mom pays Janice $2,500 per month for caregiving services. If mom moves to the nursing home in the next five years, the payments to Janice are compensation, not gifts.

Caregiver Agreements must follow strict rules, so should be drafted by an experienced elder law attorney.

The Caregiver Agreement must detail the services to be performed and the obligations of the parties. The payment is based on the going rate of caretaking in that county. Compensation is clearly delineated with hourly and yearly calculations for 24-hour personal care.

Janice must actually give the care and document her caretaking duties. Mom must actually need the care, which should be documented with a doctor's note.

To protect family relationships, it's recommended that all family members agree with the arrangement even if they are not parties to the agreement.

Janice's compensation has tax consequences. She reports the payments as ordinary income on her income tax return and pays income taxes on the amount received. In some cases, mom may be able to deduct the payments as a medical expense.

A proper Caregiver Agreement arrangement may be a valuable elder law estate planning tool in the right circumstances.

20

Medicaid Asset Protection Trusts

Long-term care insurance is the preferred option for protecting assets from nursing home costs, since it helps keep clients out of the nursing home – by paying for home care. The trend today is to "age in place." Many clients over the years were forced to spend their final days in a facility simply because they ran out of money to pay for home health aides. Additionally, for married couples, the home care option may protect the spouse from compromising their own health and finances with the heavy burden of caregiving in their later years. Too often, it is the caregiver spouse who dies first. We sometimes refer to the situation as a "perfect storm". The spouse caregiver is often in their eighties or nineties, the job is 24/7/365 and it is a very hard one.

When the client is turned down for long-term care insurance, or is unable to afford the premium, the next best option is the Medicaid Asset Protection Trust (MAPT).   Making assets joint with adult children offers no protection since Medicaid considers all of the jointly held assets to be available for the care of the ill parent, except to the extent the child can prove the amount of their actual contribution. Additionally, outright transfers to children are generally inadvisable since those assets then become exposed to the children's debts and liabilities, divorces, etc. In addition, some children spend the money, refuse to give it back when needed or die before the parent and pass those assets on to their heirs. One exception to the inadvisability of outright transfers to children is when nursing facility care is imminent or at least foreseeable. In such a case, the assistance of an elder law attorney is essential since the amounts to be transferred, the order of assets transferred and where to transfer the assets all require the advice of counsel. The object here would be to protect as much of the assets as possible and to qualify for Medicaid benefits at the earliest possible moment. These issues are discussed in Chapters 19 through 28. If someone is just getting older, can't or won't get long-term care insurance and wants to plan ahead to protect their assets, the best option is to create a Medicaid Asset Protection Trust (MAPT).

Known as an irrevocable "income only" trust, the MAPT names someone other than you or your spouse as the trustee, usually one or more adult children, and limits you to the income. The principal must be unavailable in order for it to be protected. These trusts are ideal for the family home as well as for assets the client is only taking the income from or is simply reinvesting. The client's lifestyle is not generally affected since they continue to receive their pension and Social Security checks directly, they keep the exclusive right to use and occupy the home and they preserve all the property tax exemptions on the home. The trust may sell and trade assets through the trustee. Nevertheless, the parent retains some measure of control by reserving the right to change the trustee in the event of dissatisfaction for any reason.

Transfers to the MAPT are subject to a look-back period of up to five years. This means that if assets are transferred to the MAPT, and the client needs nursing home care any time after five years have passed, the assets in the trust are protected. Nevertheless, it always pays to get started, since you get credit for the time you accumulate, even if you don't make the five years. For example, if the client needs nursing home care, say, after only four years, then they would only have to pay for the one year that's left on the look-back.

The Medicaid Asset Protection Trust is also flexible. You may sell the home, the money is paid to the trust, and the trust may buy a condominium, for example. The condo is still protected since it is owned by the trust and the five year look back does not start over since nothing was transferred to the trust. The trust simply sold one asset and purchased another, as it is permitted to do.

The trust may buy, sell and trade stocks and other assets. IRA's and other qualified plans stay out of the trust since the principal of all such retirement plans are exempt from Medicaid. These types of assets also avoid probate as they go directly to the designated beneficiaries at death.

MAPT v. Life Estate Deed

Clients often ask whether the home should be deeded to the client's adult children while retaining a life estate in the parent or whether the Medicaid Asset Protection Trust should be used to protect the asset.

While the deed with a life estate will be less costly to the client, in most cases it offers significant disadvantages when compared to the trust. First, if the home is sold prior to the death of the Medicaid recipient, the life estate value of the home will be required to be paid towards their care. If the house is rented, the net rents are payable to the nursing facility since they belong to the life tenant. Finally, the client loses a significant portion of their capital gains tax exclusion for the sale of their primary residence as they will only be entitled to a pro rata share based on the value of the life estate to the home as a whole. All of the foregoing may lead to a situation where the family finds they must maintain a vacant home for many years. Conversely, a properly drafted MAPT preserves the full capital gains tax exclusion on the primary residence and the home may be sold by the trust without obligation to make payment of any of the principal towards the client's care, assuming we have passed the look-back period.

It should be noted here that both the life estate and the irrevocable Medicaid trust will preserve the stepped-up basis in the property provided it is only sold after the death of the parent who was the owner or grantor. Upon the death of the parent, the basis for calculating the capital gains tax is stepped up from what the parent paid, plus any improvements, to what it was worth on the parent's date of death. This effectively eliminates payment of capital gains taxes on the sale of appreciated property, such as the home, after the parent dies.

MAPT Do's and Don'ts

The following is a convenient list of "Do's and Don'ts" in managing the MAPT.

Do's

- Do make all transfers to your trust, as advised by the elder law firm, in a timely manner.

- Do use trust assets for repairs, maintenance and improvements to real property in the trust.

- Do use trust assets for payment of real estate taxes and homeowner's insurance (although non-trust assets may also be used for this purpose).

- Do take dividends and income on trust assets on at least a quarterly basis (if not, they are considered additions to principal and create a five year look back on the new money not taken every year).

- Do contact the elder law firm when you wish to make a gift from the trust to any of your beneficiaries.

- Do contact the elder law firm when a grantor needs Medicaid benefits or dies.

- Do contact the elder law firm when personal or financial circumstances change significantly.

- Do contact the elder law firm if you wish to change trustees or break the trust.

- Do provide your homeowner's insurance company with a "letter of instruction", including a copy of the trust for real property transferred to the trust, to add the trustees as "additional insureds".

- Do provide your CPA or tax preparer with a "letter of instruction" regarding the trust tax return and tax deductibility of legal fees.

- Do choose your trustee carefully to avoid the expense (and unpleasantness) of having to change the trustee.

- Do contact the elder law firm if you want to refinance, take a reverse mortgage or take out a home equity loan ("HELOC") on real property in the trust.

Don'ts

- Don't use trust assets to pay telephone or utility bills.
- Don't use trust assets to pay personal expenses.

- Don't use trust assets to purchase an automobile (since all the assets in the trust will be exposed to liability if there is a car accident).

- Don't take principal or capital gains from trust assets.

- Don't transfer IRA's or 401(k)'s to the trust.

- Don't allow beneficiaries to return to the trust or the grantor any gifts made from trust assets.

- Don't make additional transfers to the trust in the future without advising the elder law estate planning firm.

21

Sheltering Income with a Pooled Trust

To qualify for community based Medicaid, meaning receiving medical care in the home, an individual cannot make more than $829 per month and a married couple cannot make more than $1,212 per month. Obviously, these minimal income standards make it very difficult to qualify for community Medicaid. However, applicants can "spend down" excess income to meet the Medicaid income requirement.

Also, an individual cannot own more than $14,550 in assets and a married couple cannot own more than $21,450 in assets.

There are two ways to spend down income. First, the applicant can reduce the income by paying for caregiving and other medical expenses. Second, the income can be reduced through the use of a "pooled income trust" where participants deposit their funds in a general trust, each with their own sub-account within the pooled trust.

A pooled trust, which is available in all states, must be run by a non-profit organization, and exists for elderly and disabled individuals for the purpose of supplementing the participants' needs beyond government benefits. In the case of people who may not qualify for community Medicaid because of excess income, the pooled trust can allow them to stay at home, also known as "aging in place."

"Special" or "supplemental needs" trusts may also be established through a pooled trust for disabled individuals under age 65 but the focus of this chapter is the use of the "pooled income trust" to keep people at home who need long-term care if their income exceeds required levels.

For example, Ralph applies for community Medicaid to allow him to stay at home and have home health aids, paid by Medicaid, to come in to assist in his care. His monthly income is $1,600, and he doesn't have excess medical costs to spend-down. He can deduct his Medicare Part B premium, his private insurance premium and $20 of income. For this purpose, we'll estimate total deductions of $260, leaving a countable net income of $1,340. From this amount, you deduct the $829 he's allowed, which results in a spend-down of $511.

When Ralph joins the pooled trust, he sends his spend-down amount of $511 to the pooled trust administrator every month. Each month, he submits to the administrator non-medical bills in his name for rent, mortgage, telephone, utilities, cable, life insurance, auto insurance, and the like. The trust pays those bills directly up to the amount he contributed. Ralph does not receive any cash. Medicaid pays for his home care on a level determined necessary by Medicaid, based on Ralph's medical needs. Assuming he is otherwise eligible for Medicaid, Ralph qualifies for community Medicaid despite his income level.

Several non-profit organizations exist that offer pooled trusts. Applying to join a pooled trust is a formal process. Costs generally include minimal start-up fees, an initial deposit and reasonable maintenance fees. Upon the death of the participant, that individual's remaining balance stays in the pooled trust to benefit other participants.

22

Long-Term Care Insurance v. Medicaid Asset Protection Trust

Long-term care insurance (LTCI) and the Medicaid Asset Protection Trust (MAPT) are often thought of an alternatives to each other. They are not. While LTCI is both a shield and a sword, the MAPT is a shield only.

LTCI protects your assets and income from the costs of care. But it has a positive effect (the sword) in that it actually pays for someone to come into your home and care for you there. The MAPT protects assets, like your home and your life savings, but it does not protect your income (pensions, social security, interest, dividends, etc.). The MAPT is solely a defensive tactic. That being said, in the event LTCI is unavailable to the client for medical or financial reasons, the MAPT is an excellent tool. There is truth in the saying that a good defense is the best offense. With the MAPT in place five years ahead of time, the client's assets are protected and Medicaid will then pay for the cost of care. While income may be protected for community care in the home, with The Pooled Income Trust (Chapter 21), for institutionalized care in a facility your income is available to pay towards your care. If you have a spouse at home, they may keep about $3,000 per month of the couple's combined income and sometimes more, depending on whose income it is -- the community spouse's or the institutionalized spouse's.

Our stated preference for clients is LTCI, if available. Most clients would prefer to "age in place" or, in other words, stay in their own home and receive home care if needed. Here, the LTCI stretches your dollars to allow you to remain in the home for years more than you might have been able to afford otherwise. If your spouse is unable to care for themselves, it allows you to call in extra help so that you do not wear yourself out acting as a caregiver in your later years. Unfortunately, studies show that spouse caregivers often die first due to the stress of caregiving.

Some clients have adopted a hybrid approach when it comes to LTCI and the MAPT. They purposely underfund the LTCI, say taking a $250/day benefit ($7,500/month) instead of a $500/day benefit ($15,000/month). They also establish the MAPT and transfer their assets to the trust. The thinking is that the $250/day will pay for the home care that they may need and want, at half the cost of the full policy. On the other hand, if they end up in a nursing home, they won't lose their assets due to the $7,500/month they may be short, and Medicaid will pick up the difference.

There are no right and wrong answers in deciding which is the best avenue to take when considering protecting your assets from the high costs of long-term care. We have found, however, that an open discussion between the client and the experienced elder law attorney, with all of the facts and circumstances on the table, often yields the most satisfactory result.

23

Veterans Benefits
for Caregiving

Veteran Affairs (VA) provides many benefits and services to veterans, their survivors and families. VA benefits are federal benefits and are provided by the U.S. Department of Veterans Affairs.

Federal Benefits

A veteran or family member may qualify for (1) VA cash assistance; (2) medical care; and (3) other benefits. The information below focuses primarily on the "cash assistance" programs available to the elderly or disabled veteran or family member.

Service Connected Compensation: This is one of the most widely known VA cash assistance programs. The fact that it is so widely known is one of the reasons many veterans don't know about, or misunderstand, other cash assistance programs that may be available to them. Service Connected Compensation benefits are paid to veterans who have a disability (or disabilities) incurred or aggravated during active military service. Based upon the degree or scope of the disability, the veteran's disability is rated in multiples of 10%, ranging from 0% to 100%. The amount of compensation paid depends upon the rating assigned. Unlike Non-service Connected Disability Pension benefits (discussed below), Service Connected Compensation is paid without regard to financial need.

Service Connected Compensation benefits are counted as income for determining eligibility for, and the amount of, benefits payable by needs-based governmental programs, such as Medicaid, Supplemental Security Income, Food Stamps, and federally assisted housing.

Non-service Connected Disability Pension: Non-service Connected Disability Pension benefits, in contrast to Service Connected Compensation, are not widely known due to the widespread belief that the veteran must have been injured during military service to receive benefits. Very few of the thousands of elderly and disabled veterans who have served during wartime are aware of these benefits. Consequently, very few elderly and disabled veterans receive these cash assistance benefits which could help keep them in their home and help them afford the cost of an assisted living facility, or minimize the erosion of assets that results from the high cost of nursing home care.

Who is Eligible?

Any veteran discharged (except those dishonorably discharged) with wartime service may be eligible for veteran benefits to help aid with the cost of long-term care expenses. The veteran must have had ninety days of active military service with at least one day of service occurring during specific war-time service periods. The geographic location where the veteran served is irrelevant. It is only the time periods in which the veteran served that is important.

Although to qualify for the program the disability does not need to be connected to the military service of the veteran, the veteran must currently suffer from permanent and total disability. The VA will generally accept a letter from the veteran's physician substantiating the disability. In lieu of the physician's letter, a support medical assessment or medical statement can be provided on V.A. Form 21-2680, obtainable from the local County Veterans Service Office.

Financial Need (Income Requirements): The general rule is that even if the veteran (or veteran's spouse or dependents) fulfills all of the above requirements, the application will be denied if the veteran's countable income exceeds the maximum annual pension rate. Countable income is all income of any kind attributable to the veteran.

In computing the income of the veteran, certain items may be deducted from income. Specifically, unreimbursed medical expenses (UME's) paid by the veteran may be used to reduce the veteran's income.

Many items constitute unreimbursed medical expenses. Included in this list are: doctor's and dentist's fees, eyeglasses, Medicare deductions, co-payments, prescriptions, transportation to doctors, therapy, health insurance and funeral expenses. Also included in unreimbursed medical expenses are the cost of the skilled nursing facility, assisted living facility or in-home aide. Obviously, these can make up a sizeable portion of the unreimbursed medical expenses.

A deduction for the medical expense can only be made if the expense has actually been paid. They must also be unreimbursed medical expenses; that is, the beneficiary will receive no payment for out-of-pocket expenses paid by the beneficiary. The unreimbursed medical expenses can be incurred by either the beneficiary or a relative of the beneficiary who lives in the same household. This person does not have to be a dependent of the veteran.

Insurance premiums paid by the beneficiary or member of the household are allowable medical expenses. Insurance includes health insurance (including Medigap policy premiums) and long-term care policies. If a physician directs a beneficiary to take nonprescription drugs, the cost of such over-the-counter medicines is an allowable medical expense deduction. Mechanical and electronic devices that compensate for a claimant's or dependent's disabilities are deductible medical expenses to the extent that they represent expenses that would not normally be incurred by non-disabled persons. Medicare premiums paid to the Social Security Administration are deducible as medical insurance premiums. The costs of an adult day care center, rest home, group home or similar facility or program is an allowable medical expense as long as the facility provides some medical or nursing services for the disabled. The services do not have to be paid to a licensed health care professional. An Alzheimer's day care program would be an example of this.

The costs of long-term care may, and often will, be the largest unreimbursed medical expense. A medical expense deduction may be allowed for unreimbursed nursing home fees even though the nursing home may not be licensed by the state to provide skilled or intermediate level care. The definition of a "nursing home" for purposes of the medical expense deduction is not the same as the definition of nursing home set forth in the federal regulations. A nursing home for the purposes of the medical expense deduction is any facility which provides extended term inpatient medical care.

In-home attendants (i.e. aides) are an allowable medical expense deduction as long as the attendant provides some medical or nursing services for the disabled person. The attendant does not have to be a licensed health professional. All reasonable fees paid to the individual for personal care of the disabled person, and maintenance of the disabled person's immediate environment, may be allowed. This includes services such as cooking and housekeeping for the disabled person. It is not necessary to distinguish between "medical" and "non-medical" services. For example, the veteran pays an attendant to administer medication and provide for the veteran's personal needs. The attendant also cooks the veteran's meals and cleans their house. The entire amount paid to the attendant may be allowed as a deductible medical expense. It makes no difference if the attendant is a licensed health professional.

The cost of an assisted living facility, nursing home and even part or all of the cost in an independent living facility may be an allowable medical deduction. The facility must show that it is providing "managed health care assistance" or "medical management". If the beneficiary is maintained in a home or other institution because he/she needs to live in a protected environment, fees paid to the institution are deductible expenses to the extent they represent payment for medical treatment. The beneficiary's doctor is your best ally in showing the need for facility care.

Financial Need (Net Worth Requirements): In addition to the income requirement, the veteran's net worth should not exceed $80,000. Assets of the veteran, or if married, the veteran and spouse, are counted with the primary residence and one vehicle being excluded.

Coordination of Federal VA Benefits with Medicaid Benefits

Usually, VA compensation and pension payments are counted as income for Medicaid eligibility purposes. The portion of the benefit that is Aid & Attendance benefits, however, is specifically excluded from the definition of income. After eligibility, if the single veteran resides in a nursing home, the Aid and Attendance pension benefit is reduced to $90, payable directly to the veteran. Married veterans can keep their Aid and Attendance for maintenance of the spouse in the marital home. The courts have disagreed as to whether payments made under other Medicaid programs would be reduced by actual payments made for Aid & Attendance. Presumably, since Aid & Attendance is excluded in the definition of income and does not fall under the $90 exception above, it should continue to be excluded for other purposes as well.

The surviving spouse of a veteran who would have been entitled to these benefits will be eligible for widow's or widower's benefits with the same criteria for income, assets and health condition.

The primary problem that arises when coordinating VA benefits with Medicaid relates to asset transfers. The VA allows for asset transfers with no look-back period whatsoever. When applying for Medicaid, all Medicaid look-back periods apply and thus a transfer that was legitimate for VA purposes may cause a period of disqualification for Medicaid purposes. There are a number of steps that can be taken to remedy the situation including, but not limited to, a return of the entire principal that was transferred should Medicaid later be needed. At that time, appropriate Medicaid planning tools and devices must then be used to again protect those assets under the Medicaid rules.

24

Applying for Medicaid

I n the event the client requires home care or institutionalized care in a nursing home facility, an application for Medicaid benefits may be required. Due to complex asset and transfer rules, the application should be made with the aid of an experienced elder law attorney. Again, it is useful in this context for a confidential survey of the client's assets, as well as any transfers of those assets, to be filled out prior to the initial consultation. This form of financial survey will be significantly different from the one used for estate planning purposes. As a combined federal and state program, Medicaid asset and transfer rules vary significantly from state to state.

There are two different kinds of Medicaid, Community Medicaid and Chronic Care Medicaid.

Community Medicaid

Community based Medicaid applications are any elderly/disabled person who wishes to remain in the community, in the setting of their own home. This benefit requires three (3) months of financial documentation, current proof of income, along with "common documents" and the past year's income tax filing, with 1099's.

Although only low income recipients may qualify for this benefit, as seen earlier in Chapter 21, any middle income person may qualify for this benefit by using The Pooled Income Trust to shelter excess income. By using The Pooled Income Trust even middle class people may become eligible for Community Medicaid.

Once benefits have been applied for and a Medicaid "pick-up" date has been established, the applicant may keep some of their monthly income and the balance is required to be contributed to their care, unless sheltered with The Pooled Income Trust. The amounts you may retain are constantly changing and are naturally different for singles and couples. Consult with an elder law attorney for the going rates in your community at any given time.

Resources, which are assets belonging to the applicant and/or community spouse, must be reported and an individual is allowed to keep only a modest amount, less than fifteen thousand dollars. If there is a spouse at home, the resource allowance may be as much as one hundred and twenty thousand dollars.

Chronic Care

Perhaps your loved one may no longer stay at home because they have become a danger to themselves or others. Maybe they need too much care or their caregiver is no longer able to manage their care. In such a case you may want to apply for chronic care benefits.

The Chronic Care application requires a look-back of five years, or sixty months. You must provide all financial statements of any open or closed accounts in this time period. Each county is different in the type of documentation you will need to present. Again, all "common documents" must be presented, five years of tax returns, proof of income, and the correct application.

The Department of Social Services will look for any gifts or transfers made in the look-back period (gifts to children, friends, grandchildren, church donations, charitable donations, etc.). Each gift will incur a penalty period determined by the state Medicaid Regional Rates chart published each year. Should you apply before the penalty period has expired you may be asked to provide additional documentation.

On all applications the county will begin an investigation. They will request an IRS report for the past five years, they will request a DMV report to see what vehicles are or were owned, they will request a financial institution report under the applicant's and his/her spouse's Social Security number and if something has not been reported the department may charge the applicant with fraud if they feel a deliberate attempt was made to hide assets.

In our experience, most individuals who attempt to file for Medicaid benefits, without the assistance of counsel, either complete the application incorrectly, do not provide the correct documentation or give unnecessary information which causes the county to investigate further. These types of errors may require an appeal, known as a Fair Hearing, to have the matter rectified.

An individual applying for chronic care benefits and who is in a nursing home is required to pay virtually all of their income towards their care. The community spouse, if there is one, is allowed to keep about three thousand dollars per month in income and, if they fall short, the institutionalized spouse is allowed to contribute some of their income to the community spouse before paying the nursing home.

In the following chapters we discuss the most common techniques used to protect assets and qualify for Medicaid.

25

Medicaid Exempt
Assets

U nder Medicaid, the combined assets of spouses are available for the care of the ill or "institutionalized" spouse, regardless whose name those assets are in.

Nevertheless, many assets or "resources" are exempt from Medicaid when there is a spouse at home (the "community spouse"). These are:

- The home up to a value of $814,000

- $75,000 to $120,000 in resources

- One automobile

- Prepaid funeral and burial for applicant and spouse

- Household furniture, personal effects, jewelry with sentimental value

- IRA's, 401(k)'s and other qualified plans, provided they are paying out a monthly income

- Annuities paying out a monthly income naming spouse as primary beneficiary

- Medicaid Asset Protection Trust (MAPT) assets, if held in trust more than five years

- Assets in trusts set up by someone other than the applicant

- Supplemental Needs Trusts (also known as "Special Needs Trusts") for the benefit of a disabled person under age sixty-five

- Pooled Income Trusts for disabled persons subject to county DSS approval

The above exemptions create some planning opportunities. Should the Medicaid applicant have a disabled child or grandchild, they can immediately protect any assets they choose to place into a Special Needs Trust for the child or grandchild.

Since the home is an exempt asset when a spouse is living there, so are repairs and improvements to the home, including new carpeting, appliances, kitchen, baths, modifications for handicapped accessibility, lifts for stairs, etc. A mortgage can be paid off to reduce the amount of assets required to be "spent down" in order to obtain Medicaid eligibility. Although only one automobile is allowed, nothing prevents the spouse from trading in the old clunker for a brand new car.

When there is no spouse, the resource allowance falls to about $15,000. The home and automobile, no longer needed by the applicant, are no longer exempt. Nevertheless, the home may still be protected if an adult child was living in the home and caring for the parent for the two year period immediately prior to the parent entering the nursing home under the "primary caregiver" rule. Care in this context is interpreted broadly. The home may also be protected if a sibling of the applicant lived in the home for at least one year and has an "equity interest", the latter term also being broadly interpreted. All of the other exemptions listed above, if there is a spouse, also apply if there is no spouse.

Income exemptions also depend on whether or not there is a spouse. For nursing home care, the community spouse may keep about three thousand per month of the couple's income. In the case where the spouse's income exceeds the threshold, the spouse may keep most of his or her own excess income as well. The rules also allow keeping greater "resources" to generate the income necessary to meet the exemption, if the income is not otherwise available, although this must be applied for. Veterans' "Aid and Attendance" benefits are also exempt.

Clients often ask whether Medicaid can "go after" the assets when the community spouse dies after the institutionalized spouse. If the assets were exempt, then Medicaid has no "right of recovery" since Medicaid was properly paid. However, if assets are left by will to a surviving institutionalized spouse, Medicaid will assert a claim. If the assets were left to someone other than the spouse, Medicaid may seek to exercise the institutionalized spouse's "right of election" since spouses are entitled to claim a share of the estate if they are disinherited. Proper planning with an elder law attorney can avoid these unfortunate results.

26

Medicaid Annuities to Protect Assets

M edicaid annuities have been a viable planning option for spouses since The Deficit Reduction Act of 2005.

Say you have a spouse who needs nursing home care (the "institutionalized spouse") but you have more assets than the Medicaid law allows you, the spouse at home (the "community spouse") to keep. Currently, the community spouse may keep up to about $120,000 in resources (not including the house, which is exempt if a spouse is living there up to about $800,000 in equity). But what if the couple has $400,000 in assets? That's $280,000 in excess resources.

Many well meaning advisers, including lawyers, will tell you that it is too late and you have to first spend down that $280,000 before

Medicaid will pay. This is incorrect advice.

Elder law attorneys have a number of good planning options here, such as "spousal refusal" and the "gift and loan" strategy, discussed in subsequent chapters. Another planning option, the Medicaid annuity, may in some cases turn out to be the best planning option.

The community spouse purchases a Medicaid annuity worth the excess $280,000, which annuity must make repayments of the full amount of the annuity plus interest within the community spouse's actuarial life expectancy. Now, the $280,000 has disappeared and the institutionalized spouse is immediately eligible for Medicaid, saving nursing home costs of sometimes $15,000 or more per month. Spouse at home also receives an increased income which is also almost all sheltered from Medicaid.

27

Spousal Refusal – "Just Say No"

Spousal refusal is a legally valid Medicaid planning option in just three states: New York, Florida and Connecticut. By way of background, certain income and assets are exempt from Medicaid if there is a spouse. Generally, the spouse at home, known as the "community spouse" may keep about $3,000 per month of the couple's combined income and up to about $120,000 of the assets or "resources". Not included in those figures are any other exempt assets, such as a home and one automobile. The spouse who is being cared for in a facility is known as the "institutionalized spouse".

Many a spouse has advised us that they simply cannot afford to live on the allowances that Medicaid provides. This is where spousal refusal comes in. We start by shifting excess assets into the name of the community spouse. He or she then signs a document which the elder law attorney prepares and files with the Department of Social Services (DSS) indicating that they refuse to contribute their income and assets to the care of the ill spouse since they need those income and assets for their own care and well-being. Note that you may not refuse your spouse's own income over the $3,000 per month exemption as it is not coming to you.

Once the community spouse invokes their right to refuse, and all of the other myriad requirements of the Medicaid application are met, the state Medicaid program must pay for the care of the institutionalized spouse.

After Medicaid has been granted, DSS may institute a lawsuit seeking to recover the cost of care from the refusing spouse. Nevertheless, there are a few reasons why spousal refusal makes sense, even in light of this risk. First, in many instances, DSS never invokes this right. Secondly, these lawsuits are often settled for significantly less than the cost of care provided. Thirdly, the payment to the county can sometimes be deferred until the community spouse dies. As one county attorney told us when agreeing to such an arrangement, "the county is going to be around for a long time". Finally, even though the county may seek recovery, it is only for the Medicaid reimbursement rate and not the private pay rate. For example, if the private pay rate is $15,000 per month, which is what you would have to pay, the amount Medicaid has to pay is much less in most cases. So the Medicaid rate at the same facility may be only $10,000 per month. The county may only pursue you for the amount they actually paid. Worst case scenario then, if you had to repay the county, is that you would still be saving $5,000 per month for the cost of your spouse's care.

Spousal refusal is an excellent option for spouses who find one of them on the nursing home doorstep. Far better, however, is to plan ahead with long-term care insurance or, where such insurance is not available for medical or financial reasons, consider setting up a Medicaid Asset Protection Trust (MAPT) at least five years ahead of time to protect your home and life savings.

28

Saving Half on the Nursing Home Doorstep: The "Gift and Loan" Strategy

What do you do when a client comes in to see you and says that his mother is going into a nursing home and she has $300,000 in assets. In fact, mom scrimped and saved all of her life to have this nest egg and now she desperately wants to see her children get an inheritance.

Although you may protect all of your assets by planning five years ahead of time with a Medicaid Asset Protection Trust, all is not lost if nothing has been done and the client finds herself on the nursing home doorstep.

The advanced elder law technique, used to protect assets at the last minute, is called the "gift and loan" strategy. Here's how it works. Let's assume, for the purposes of our example, that the nursing home costs $15,000 a month. When mom goes into the nursing home, we gift one-half of the nest egg, in this case one-half of $300,000, or $150,000, to her children. Then we lend the other $150,000 to the children and they execute a promissory note agreeing to repay the $150,000 in ten monthly payments of $15,000 per month, together with a modest amount of interest. Now we apply for Medicaid benefits. Medicaid will impose a penalty period (i.e., they will refuse to pay) for 10 months on the grounds that the gift of $150,000 could have been used to pay for mom's care for 10 months. Medicaid ignores the loan since it was not a gift. It is going to be paid back, with interest, according to the terms of the promissory note. What happens is that the ten loan repayment installments will be used to pay for mom's nursing home care during the penalty period. Just when the loan repayments are finished, the penalty period expires and Medicaid begins to pick up the tab. Lo and behold, the children get to keep the $150,000 gift and mom has saved some of the inheritance for her children.

Also known as "half-a-loaf planning", this technique has been approved in most states. And, of course, everyone knows what half-a-loaf is better than, right?

Estate Administration
Upon Death

29

Estate Administration and Probate

Probate is the legal proceeding in which the probate court assumes jurisdiction over the assets of someone who has died. The court supervises the payment of debts, taxes, and probate fees, and then supervises the distribution of the remainder to the persons named in a will, or to the legal heirs if there is no will. Probate may not be necessary if a deceased person had a properly drafted and funded trust. However, trust administration is necessary.

Family members commonly believe that their deceased loved one properly planned because the decedent had a will, had created and funded a trust, or had designated certain individuals as beneficiaries. In fact, sometimes the decedent's plans may actually have a negative impact on the family with regard to estate taxes, and/or Medicaid planning strategies for the surviving spouse. If this occurs, experienced elder law estate planning attorneys can advise you about post-mortem planning techniques that may rectify the situation and create more favorable tax consequences for surviving family members. Assets that were "exempt" for Medicaid while the spouse was living may now be "available", such as the home. It is always a good idea to review the estate plan after the first spouse dies.

Unlike a will, a trust is a private document and need not be filed with the probate court on death. Nonetheless, the successor trustee must still take steps to administer the trust: beneficiaries must be contacted and kept informed; the grantor's assets gathered and invested; any debts paid; potential creditors notified; taxes filed and paid; assets and/or income distributed in conformity with trust provisions to beneficiaries, etc.

Successor trustees often lack the time, resources or knowledge to personally administer the trust, and therefore may call upon legal, accounting and investment professionals for assistance.

Successor Trustee's Obligations

Below is a summary of the basic obligations of a successor trustee of a trust.

Show loyalty to all trust beneficiaries. Even if the successor trustee is himself a beneficiary, as trustee he has the duty of loyalty to all the other beneficiaries, including the contingent beneficiaries.

Deal impartially with beneficiaries. The successor trustee may not favor the lifetime income beneficiary over the interests of the remainder beneficiaries who will take after the death of the lifetime beneficiary. Investments must balance the need for income with the requirement for growth.

Make the trust property productive of income. This duty is violated if the successor trustee keeps large amounts in a checking account that does not pay interest and does not grow in value. There may be other trust assets which do not produce income, such as a vacant home. These assets must be disposed of or made productive within a reasonable time, since they are considered "wasting" assets which deplete the estate. The trustee may be liable for failing to convert "wasting" assets into productive assets.

Invest only in prudent investments. The prudent investor rule requires:

- Consideration by the trustee of the purposes, terms and other circumstances of the trust.

- Exercise reasonable care and caution as part of an overall investment strategy which incorporates risk and return objectives reasonably suitable to the trust.

- Diversity of investments, unless specific reasons are present not to diversify.

- Review and implementation of a formal investment plan.

- An investment strategy that considers both the reasonable production of income and safety of principal, consistent with the fiduciary's duty of impartiality towards the beneficiaries and the purposes of the trust.

Account to beneficiaries and keep beneficiaries informed. Upon commencement of the trust administration, the successor trustee must inform all income and remainder beneficiaries of his acceptance of the trust. If a beneficiary requests it, the successor trustee is required to provide that beneficiary with a complete copy of the trust document, including any amendments as well as relevant information about the assets of the trust and the particulars relating to administration. In addition, even without request, all beneficiaries must be provided with an annual statement of the accounts of the trust.

Keep trust assets separate. The successor trustee must keep the assets of each trust separate and keep his personal assets separate from the trust assets. This requires separate bank accounts, brokerage accounts, and safe deposit boxes for trust assets. It is particularly important that you keep the assets of the deceased spouse's Credit Shelter Trust (also known as the AB Trust or Bypass Trust), if they had one, separate from all other assets, since these assets will pass tax-free at the death of the surviving spouse. If the surviving spouse, acting as trustee, comingles any other assets in with these assets (or even simply takes the assets out of the trust and mixes them with her personal assets), in addition to breaching fiduciary obligations, the successor trustee will have subjected these otherwise exempt assets to taxation when she dies.

Avoid conflicts of interest and self dealing. The successor trustee cannot buy assets from the trust or sell his personal assets to the trust. He cannot favor himself as a beneficiary at the expense of any other remainder or potential remainder beneficiary. He cannot make any distribution to anyone or any withdrawals from the trust unless specifically authorized by the trust to do so. Conflicts of interest and self-dealing are often vague and ill-defined. If you are a trustee and have any concern as to any specific action or situation, consult with an experienced attorney.

Preserve the trust assets and uphold the trust. The successor trustee is liable if trust assets are lost, misplaced or destroyed because of inattention or negligence. The successor trustee should always be certain that all trust assets are appropriately protected and insured.

File tax returns and pay any tax due. Each trust has a tax year, which like the personal tax year, ends annually on December 31. The trust must have a taxpayer identification number and file a tax return no later than April 15 of the year following. The income tax return for the trust is Form 1041, the Fiduciary Income Tax Return. If this is not filed annually and timely, penalties and interest may be assessed. There may be other tax returns and taxes, like the decedent's personal tax return, which the trust may be required to file, and the successor trustee is responsible for doing so.

We recommend that successor trustees consult with a qualified and experienced Certified Public Accountant. You should not assume that your long-time CPA is necessarily experienced or qualified, since fiduciary taxation differs significantly from taxation of individuals and corporations, the types of accounting that CPA's are generally most familiar with. Before deciding on a CPA for the trust, determine whether that individual has experience and qualifications in this specialized area.

Distribute income. Income generally includes interest earned on bank accounts, CD's, bonds or mortgages, and dividends on stocks and mutual funds. The current income beneficiaries are entitled to all of the income annually. Beneficiaries cannot choose to take less than all of the income, and the trustee is under an obligation to distribute it. Certain types of income may also consist of principal as well as income. If this is the case, the portion that is income is distributed and the portion that is principal is retained. If there is any question about what is principal and what is income, consult with the trust's CPA.

Handle trust expenses. The administration of the trust necessarily requires certain expenditures. Example of expenses include CPA fees, legal services, the cost of insurance or real estate taxes on real estate owned by the trust. Every check written by the successor trustee (except to pay trust income) and each direct charge to a trust's bank or brokerage account, is considered a trust expense. Like receipts, expenses must also be appropriately apportioned between the income side and the principal side.

Delegate investment functions if necessary. In many instances, individual trustees are not equipped to comply with their investment responsibilities. In these cases, investment professionals may be retained. The successor trustee is obligated to exercise reasonable care, judgment and caution in selecting an investment agent. Trust administration specialists may be found through brokerage houses, banks and some law firms. Note that "delegating" differs from merely obtaining investment advice. It contemplates turning over the investment functions to an advisor as opposed to simply seeking advice, and then acting or not acting on that advice. Even if investment functions are fully turned over to an agent, the successor trustee is still required to monitor the agent's investment performance.

A successor trustee should not assume that he has satisfied his investment responsibilities just because he has consulted regularly or occasionally with a stockbroker. Further, stockbrokers are often unaware of the prudent investor rule and fiduciary duties of a successor trustee.

Good record keeping. Keeping accurate, up-to-date and comprehensive records is one of the most difficult jobs a successor trustee must perform. If the successor trustee becomes disabled or dies, another person must be able to seamlessly step into his shoes and understand the current status of trust matters. Trust records are also vital because the trustee must be able to explain any trust matter if the IRS or remainder beneficiary requests it. The CPA selected to handle the trust can be very helpful in setting up a sound accounting and record-keeping system. If keeping records is too burdensome for the successor trustee, he can retain the trust department of a bank, the CPA or the law firm to do the work on a fee basis.

30

Trustee's Duties
Upon the Death of the Grantor

Here's a "to do" list, including both legal and practical responsibilities, of the trustee upon the death of the grantor.

• Locate and review all of the deceased's important papers. Sometimes directions for funeral and other pertinent information may be located in the deceased's papers, so these documents should be reviewed as quickly as possible.

• If the deceased was living alone, change locks and take any steps necessary to close the house. If the house will be vacant, insurance carriers should be notified of this fact. Check on auto and property insurance to be certain trust assets are insured against loss or liability.

• Obtain certified copies of the death certificate from the funeral director, or the city, town or village clerk where the death occurred.

• Make a list of all household goods to be distributed to beneficiaries. To be absolutely safe, if several beneficiaries are involved, photograph personal property and take an unrelated, disinterested witness along when you make your list.

• Create a complete list of all assets and establish the value of those assets. The value at the time of death determines the new tax basis of appreciated assets, since all capital gains on assets is forgiven upon death. Even if the real estate, stock, or any other appreciated asset is not sold immediately, establishing a fair market value as of date of death is necessary to establish the new tax basis for future appreciation purposes, to determine whether state or federal estate tax is an issue, and to equitably distribute assets to beneficiaries as provided in the trust agreement.

• If several different accounts exist, it simplifies things greatly if liquid assets are consolidated into one account (or one savings and one checking account). That way, the check register for the account becomes a record of bills paid, deposits made or any other trust activity. As trustee, you are responsible for safeguarding the funds for the beneficiaries.

• Pay outstanding bills or debts. If the trustee does not pay bills, he or she may be held personally liable.

• If the trust will generate more than $600 in income from the date of death until all trust assets are distributed (which is generally the case), a tax identification number needs to be obtained for the trust. Where the grantor was their own trustee, their social security number was the tax identification number and the trust income was simply reported on their annual 1040 tax return. But in an irrevocable trust (which is the case where the grantor of a revocable trust dies), the trust is required to report income under its own tax identification number. In a revocable trust, for the year of death, income earned from January 1 through date of death will be reported on the grantor's final Form 1040. Income earned from date of death to date of distribution of all assets will be reported on a Form 1041.

• Be certain that all required tax returns are filed. If the deceased's state of residence has an estate tax, an estate tax return may be necessary. A Federal estate tax return may also be necessary for larger estates. If significant lifetime gifts were made, estate tax returns may also be required.

• File any claims for life insurance, IRA's and other assets needing claims forms. Liquidate any assets that need to be liquidated. Make sure to get professional advice before retitling or liquidating IRA's as there may be serious tax consequences if you make a mistake in this area.

• Create an accounting which begins with the inventory listing all assets existing on the date of death, show all additions of any type, subtract all expenses paid, and show current assets on hand. When you are ready to create the final accounting right before distribution of assets to beneficiaries, it is easiest if assets are placed in a non-interest bearing account. That way values are not constantly changing.

• Have a legal professional prepare a receipt and release form for each beneficiary to sign, simply stating that they have received the inheritance and that they release the trustee from further responsibility or liability.

• Settlement of a trust is easier than going through the probate process since court paperwork and proceedings are avoided. The trustee can access accounts immediately, so debts and expenses may be satisfied without delay and accounts may be consolidated. Most statutory waiting periods are also avoided. Real estate may be listed for sale immediately, as opposed to waiting for months and sometimes years for an executor to be appointed under a will. However, even with a trust, it is very important that specific steps be completed. It is not feasible to list here all steps which would need to be completed in each circumstance. Legal help in designing and terminating trusts streamlines the process, and saves time and money by taking advantage of all tax planning opportunities available to you.

"Joint adventurers, like copartners, owe to one another, while the enterprise continues, the duty of the finest loyalty. Many forms of conduct permissible in a workaday world for those acting at arm's length, are forbidden to those bound by fiduciary ties. A trustee is held to something stricter than the morals of the market place. Not honesty alone, but the punctilio of an honor the most sensitive, is then the standard of behavior. As to this there has developed a tradition that is unbending and inveterate. Uncompromising rigidity has been the attitude of courts of equity when petitioned to undermine the rule of undivided loyalty by the "disintegrating erosion" of particular exceptions...Only thus has the level of conduct for fiduciaries been kept at a level higher than that trodden by the crowd. It will not consciously be lowered by any judgment of this court."

Benjamin N. Cardozo, Meinhard v. Salmon,
249 N.Y. 458, 463-64, 164 N.E. 545 (1928)

31

Using a Professional Trustee
to Settle the Estate

M ost people who set up living trusts today choose themselves as trustee. However, since trusts continue after the death or disability of the original trustee, a successor trustee must be named. Should you choose an individual trustee, a professional trustee (such as a bank, lawyer or trust company) or a combination of the two?

The advantages of naming an individual are that you know the person and they know you. Presumably, they would act in your best interests knowing how you would wish diverse matters to be handled, including the investment and distribution of your trust assets.

On the other hand, managing a trust may be a complex task. Balancing the income needs of a current beneficiary with the requirement to preserve the capital for future, or contingent, beneficiaries requires knowledge of sound, conservative investment practices. In addition, annual fiduciary returns must be filed for the trust. Individuals often face other commitments or may become disabled or die, leaving the management of the trust in limbo for an extended period of time. Individual trustees may have or develop personality conflicts with siblings. We have seen unresolved childhood conflicts, dormant for years, suddenly reappear with great force in the emotional period following the death of a parent. The issues of money and control often add to these hidden problems. In a similar vein, individual trustees are subject to the influences of their spouses who may be pursuing their own agenda and who are not bound by the "family glue".

Despite parents' best intentions, the chosen trustee may act dishonestly or to their own benefit (self-dealing) and to the detriment of the other trust beneficiaries. Unlike professional trustees, they are not subject to professional or governmental oversight of their actions and they may not have the resources to right a wrong even if they are successfully sued for any wrongful acts.

For continuity, and out of respect for the grantor's choice, the professional trustee will usually retain the attorney or law firm that prepared the trust to settle the estate. The parent's law firm, as opposed to the personal lawyer of one of the children, is more likely to look after the interests of all the beneficiaries in an even-handed manner.

Conclusion

Look at all that is involved in elder law estate planning, such as using trusts for the advantages on disability and death, second marriage planning, Inheritance Trusts to protect assets from children's divorces and creditors and keep those assets in the blood, and the myriad other issues discussed in the foregoing chapters on Elder Law Estate Planning. Then look at the many issues addressed in the chapters on Medicaid Planning Strategies, so essential to protect oneself from losing one's home and life savings in the event nursing home care is needed.

How then can it be that so many attorneys practice in one of these areas while knowing little of the other? It is the premise of this book that they cannot continue to do so and properly service their middle class clients. For this reason, we have formed the American Association of Elder Law Estate Planning Attorneys (AAELEPA). The goal of AAELEPA is to develop a cadre of "ambidextrous" attorneys, equally at home in estate planning and elder law, so that the millions of Americans who get estate plans will have knowledgeable lawyers to protect their assets ahead of time as they become older – by reviewing their plans every three years as we recommend, and then installing asset protection devices, such as the Medicaid Asset Protection Trust, when the need arises. These attorneys will also provide safe harbor when nursing home care is imminent and significant assets remain exposed.

On the other hand, just because a client only comes into the planning arena late in life, through the elder law attorney, when asset protection is needed, does not mean they have to be shortchanged in their wishes to avoid probate or a will contest, to keep assets in the blood and to see to it that their assets go to whom they want, when they want, in the way they want.

We recently conversed with a fine estate planning attorney, practicing for over thirty years, with thousands of clients. He was embarrassed to admit that he knew little elder law and that he had done a disservice to so many for so long. He agreed to become a "poster child" for the newly formed association, AAELEPA. To this we say "bravo" and that the time has come for elder law estate planning to go mainstream. It is what virtually every family needs, not only the select few that we have been privileged to serve over the years.

Appendix A

Appendix A

Glossary of Elder Law Estate Planning Terms

Ancillary Probate: Term for probate if decedent had real property in another state.

Annual Exclusion: The amount of property the IRS allows a person to gift to another person during a calendar year before a gift tax is assessed and/or a gift tax return must be filed. The amount is increased periodically. There is no limit to the number of people you can give gifts to which qualify for the annual exclusion.

Assets: All types of property which can be made available for the payment of debts.

Basic/Simple Will: A will that leaves everything to your spouse upon your death, if living, otherwise in equal shares to your children.

Beneficiary: A person (or institution) who derives benefit from either the creation of a trust, proceeds of an insurance policy, or property designated by a will.

Credit Shelter Trust: A trust designed to save the personal estate tax exemption of each spouse while allowing the surviving spouse to have use of the assets of the deceased spouse during the remainder of their lifetime.

Estate: An individual's property and assets, including real estate, bank accounts, stocks, investment accounts, annuities, life insurance, IRA's and other qualified plans, as well as personal property such as automobiles and jewelry.

Estate Tax: A tax that is imposed upon a person's death, based upon the value of the estate.

Executor: A person named in a will who is authorized to manage the estate of a deceased person.

Grantor: The individual who establishes a trust (also known as "trustor" or "settlor").

Health Care Proxy: A document appointing an agent to make medical decisions for you if you are unable to communicate your own medical decisions.

Inheritance Trust: A stand-alone trust which is created to hold a beneficiary's share of their inheritance, offering them protection from creditors, lawsuits and divorces.

Living Will: A document which expresses your desire not to be kept alive by medical life-support systems in the event of a terminal illness, and authorizes withdrawal of life support by your agent.

Medicaid: A joint federal and state "needs-based" medical insurance program administered by the state to provide payment for health care services, including long-term care.

Medicaid Asset Protection Trust: A trust created during the Grantor's lifetime to hold assets in order to make them inaccessible for the expense of long-term care and nursing home costs. The Grantor is limited to access only the income generated from the trust.

Medicare: A U.S. government health insurance plan that provides hospital, medical, and surgical benefits for persons age 65 and older and people with certain disabilities.

Pour-Over Will: A document which states that any property left outside of a living trust that does not have specified beneficiaries be poured into a living trust and distributed to the trust beneficiaries.

Power of Attorney: A document appointing an agent to make legal, business, financial and certain other personal decisions for you.

Probate: The legal process in which a court oversees the distribution of property left in a will.

Revocable Living Trust: A trust created during the grantor's lifetime to hold assets during that person's lifetime, passing assets to the trust beneficiaries on death without the expense and delay of probate proceedings.

Special Needs Trust (SNT): A trust which enables a person with a disability to maintain eligibility for government benefits [for example, Medicaid and Supplemental Security Income (SSI)]. The purpose of the trust is to enhance the quality of life for the disabled person. These trusts are also called "Supplementary Needs Trusts".

Made in the USA
Middletown, DE
06 May 2015